Groundhog Day
in West Virginia

1 Thess 5:16-18

Mary Feuchtenberger

Mary Feuchtenberger

Copyright © 2016 Mary Feuchtenberger.

All rights reserved. No part of this book may be reproduced, stored, or transmitted by any means—whether auditory, graphic, mechanical, or electronic—without written permission of both publisher and author, except in the case of brief excerpts used in critical articles and reviews. Unauthorized reproduction of any part of this work is illegal and is punishable by law.

Scripture taken from the Contemporary English Version © 1991, 1992, 1995 by American Bible Society, Used by Permission.

Scripture taken from the Holman Christian Standard Bible ® Copyright © 2003, 2002, 2000, 1999 by Holman Bible Publishers. All rights reserved.

Scripture taken from the New King James Version. Copyright © 1979, 1980, 1982 by Thomas Nelson, Inc. Used by permission. All rights reserved.

Scripture taken from the King James Version of the Bible.

Scripture taken from the Holy Bible, NEW INTERNATIONAL VERSION®. Copyright © 1973, 1978, 1984 by Biblica, Inc. All rights reserved worldwide. Used by permission. NEW INTERNATIONAL VERSION® and NIV® are registered trademarks of Biblica, Inc. Use of either trademark for the offering of goods or services requires the prior written consent of Biblica US, Inc.

All Scripture quotations in this publications are from The Message. Copyright © by Eugene H. Peterson 1993, 1994, 1995, 1996, 2000, 2001, 2002. Used by permission of NavPress Publishing Group.

ISBN: 978-1-4834-4431-4 (sc)
ISBN: 978-1-4834-4430-7 (e)

Because of the dynamic nature of the Internet, any web addresses or links contained in this book may have changed since publication and may no longer be valid. The views expressed in this work are solely those of the author and do not necessarily reflect the views of the publisher, and the publisher hereby disclaims any responsibility for them.

Any people depicted in stock imagery provided by Thinkstock are models, and such images are being used for illustrative purposes only. Certain stock imagery © Thinkstock.

Lulu Publishing Services rev. date: 01/21/2016

CONTENTS

Acknowledgments vii
The Beginning ix

Notes 1   (Difficulties) 1
Notes 2   (Back to Russell) 17
Notes 3   (Hank) 23
Notes 4   (Growing Up) 30
Notes 5   (Mother) 38
Notes 6   (Russell) 41
Notes 7   (Prayer) 49
Notes 8   (Letter) 53
Notes 9   (Blessings) 55
Notes 10 (Travel) 60
Notes 11 (Letters) 65
Notes 12 (Family) 68
Notes 13 (Jail) 71
Notes 14 (Decline) 76
Notes 15 (Beth's Letters) 83
Notes 16 (Change) 91
Notes 17 (Recreation) 96
Notes 18 (Rehab) 102
Notes 19 (Cousins) 106
Notes 20 (Texas) 112
Notes 21 (Discord) 123
Notes 22 (KABOOM) 127

Notes 23 (Home).. 132
Notes 24 (Princeton) 141
Notes 25 (Red Moon) 146
Notes 26 (Social media)... 151
Notes 27 (Lace) 153
Notes 28 (Granny) 155
Notes 29 (Heroes) 158
Notes 30 (Groundhog Day) 161

Epilogue.. 163
About The Author 165

ACKNOWLEDGMENTS

I am having that closer walk with God through the use of my cell phone, various apps, and Goggle, the Bible, hymns, and several books while putting my words in my phone notebook.

I have actually typed the entire book on my phone over the course of a year and a half. I have the Holy Bible app and have used different versions of Bible verses as follows:

CEV Contemporary English Version
HCSB Holman Christian Standard Bible
KJV King James Version
MSG The Message
NIV New International Version
NKJV New King James Version

Occasionally, I have summarized Bible verses in my own words.

Goggle has led me to Wikipedia Free Encyclopedia for much of my information, as well as to library.timelesstruths.org which has provided words to hymns. YouTube enables me to enjoy many hymns by various artists.

The Bluefield Daily Telegraph, Bluefield WV was used for two passages.

I read a copy of Corrie ten Boom's the Hiding Place many years ago and recently read Unbroken by Laura Hillenbrand. Both books are inspiring. The most inspiring book, though, is A Purpose Driven Life by Rick Warren.

My sister-in-law Betse has helped me immensely with proof reading and suggestions. Thank you Betse, and thank you God for giving me a sister by marriage.

Social media has been a wonderful source of information with daily Christian messages, hymns, Bible verses, and postings of faith. Messages of many have also been shared. Three of my daughter's letters to her son Russell are included and a few family emails.

All of this has enriched my life. Possibly, some of my memories are dimmed by time. Hopefully, no one will object to my version of events, but please accept my apology if discrepancies occur.

THE BEGINNING

Early in March of 2014, I text Russell, "I am writing about you to show that prayer can help people to get off drugs." His response, "Are you going to get it published?" As I continued to write, the book became about more than Russell. Much of it discusses becoming close to God and the importance of living a Christian life. Then, I began to think of my life in West Virginia and of family and friends, and I expanded my writing to include childhood memories.

I read Colossians 3:23 (NIV) **"Whatever you do, work at it with all your heart, as working for The Lord."** I have worked with all my heart and would love to publish this book to help people in their walk with God, but if it is never read, I can honestly say that it has brought me much closer to God. Our personal walk with Him is of upmost importance! I have searched scripture and hymns and reaped tremendous rewards. His spirit is with me, and I can feel it throughout the day. Many times in my writings, I will mention that I am crying, and tears can be good. Some of the best moments come when listening to a hymn or reading the lyrics of a hymn. Social media has been a marvelous source of inspiration with Christian messages, Bible verses and hymns posted most ever day. I just listened to "How Great Thou Art" on my phone and cried, with joy!

After writing that last sentence, I went to the funeral of a 96 year old church member. It was a fabulous service with many people in attendance! I never thought of a funeral as being something I would want to observe, but now I realize what a blessing it can be. Four people chose to speak of the goodness of this man, and two people sang hymns. It became a joyous occasion, as we were reminded of his Christian devotion and of some of the humor in his life. We know that he is in Heaven now, and that knowledge brings peace. The church music was awesome, and our pastor sang How Great Thou Art, so I got to hear this amazing hymn once more. It was perfect and caused my tears to fall, with joy!

Again, we recently attended services for my husband's Aunt. It was a splendid event! Her granddaughter, through tears, told of the loving and caring person she was. Many family members and friends spoke of her goodness and recalled life events. What an honor to be a part of this celebration! Many could learn from this example. My own Aunt Lucille had a joyous funeral years ago. I was amazed at how much we laughed and how happy we were. Her daughter Sandra spoke of numerous events in her life, and we responded with much laughter. Her son John played the flute, and we listened to one of her favorite songs--Operator, Get Me Jesus on the Telephone. In my mind, there is no better way to leave this earth than to have a fabulous celebration to honor a child of our Almighty God! I pray that each of us will be blessed with His Holy Spirit as we walk this earth in preparation for eternity!

Notes 1
(Difficulties)

Sometimes we may wonder why defiant people and combative situations are in our lives. We reason that it would be wonderful to have a life that is smooth sailing, like the lives of many people we know or think that we know. I have wished countless times for that easy highway, but soon realized that there is value in the drama that comes, seemingly from nowhere, to ruin my peaceful road. Do you know someone who is using drugs and the chaos that comes with addiction? It appears that most everyone today has a family member or friend involved in illegal drug use or legal drug or alcohol abuse. I became totally worn out with our family druggie, and finally it got to the point where I honestly didn't care. Prayer after prayer went unanswered, and I said that he would just have to pray for himself. And, I also said that he could go to hell! I had dealt with more than enough!!!

But as I began to think about him, the love I felt came back, and I petitioned God for him. We, his grandparents, went for counseling with our pastor, and put him on the church prayer list. All of our family and friends were asked for prayer. We went forward in church and had the elders gather around us and pray, and we asked anyone and everyone for advice. Countless hours were spent scouring the internet for information on drug treatment and solutions for addiction and the experiences of other people. We were not going to allow the devil to have him. That was not an option! There are numerous obstacles to overcome to rescue a person on drugs. It is not easy and requires much time and ongoing effort. Many times they backslide. But, everyone can help their loved one if they will follow God's word. Addiction is a disease!

My goal is to bring my grandson to God, so that he can receive our Savior's help. How much time, and how much energy are you willing to use to rescue your lost sheep? From the Bible NKJV Luke 15:4-7, **"What man of you, having a hundred sheep, if he loses one of them, does not leave the ninety-nine in the wilderness, and go after the one which is lost until he finds it? And when he has found it, he lays it on his shoulders, rejoicing. And when he comes home, he calls together his friends and neighbors, saying to them, "Rejoice with me; for I have found my sheep which was lost!" I say to you, that likewise there will be more joy in heaven over one sinner who repents than over ninety- nine just persons who need no repentance."**

Psalms 23, written by the shepherd David before he became King, is wonderfully explained by Kerry and Chris Shook at kerryshook.org. They explain how desperately sheep need a shepherd and how that applies to us. I was surprised to learn that sheep will eat every bit of vegetation in one area and be too dumb to move on. A shepherd needs a staff to herd and correct them and sometimes a rod to protect them. Sheep are totally dependent on their shepherd AS ARE WE! Without Him we may not move in the right direction and may make wrong decisions. God, our shepherd, provides all of our needs. NKJV Psalm 23 **Verse 1 "The Lord is my shepherd; I shall not want."** (So, we will be taken care of by Him and will not want or have need). Verse 2-3 **"He makes me lie down in green pastures; He leads me beside the still waters."** (Take time to be quiet and slow down from busy schedules, and also have peace through Christ in all that you do**). "He restores my soul;" Verse 5 "You prepare a table before me in the presence of my enemies."** Chris and Kerry say that we need to slow down and be nourished by God. He protects us! Give the Creator of the universe some quiet quality time!

Russell is the grandson that I didn't want. His mother, Beth, my only daughter, began dating Russell's Dad, Hank, when she was 15. Beth was an honor roll student and a hard worker. She had Christian values and knew The Lord, but as a young teen was not yet fully committed to Christian living. She already had a good work ethic. When I wouldn't buy an expensive sweater for her, and, jokingly, told her to get a job...she did! We had to go to the board of education and get a work permit since she was only 14, 2 months shy of her 15th birthday. We both were shocked that the local Dairy Queen would hire her. I think that she admitted to being 15, almost 16, and they didn't do the math.

Anyway, she maintained her good grades and seemed happy to be working and having money to spend. She started tenth grade, her first year at the high school. Working limited school activities, but she didn't seem to mind. She had already run the gamut of sports in elementary and junior high. She had taken dance lessons with Janis for several years and enjoyed the end of year performances, once as the lead in Hansel and Gretel. At age 8 she took swim lessons, joined the swim team, and had much success. The camaraderie was great, and many ribbons and trophies honored her achievements. Soccer was her next game of choice and required much physical skill and determination. Later, she joined the track team, mostly, I think, to be with the athletes. She enjoyed being a cheer leader in ninth grade, but wasn't interested in trying out the next year. In between activities, she had many girl friends. Julie, Kim, Robin and Leah are a few of the treasured friends who spent time in our home. And, Wendy will always be a very important person in our lives, but now lives far away in Miami with her husband Pablo.

In ninth grade Beth was elected homecoming queen, and Kevin Sizemore was elected King. He is presently a busy actor in Hollywood, as is his son Gunnar, and his wife Gina Lombardi is a fitness expert. Kevin is currently seen in the acclaimed movie *Woodlawn* which is encouraging many to live a Christian life, and the best thing about

Mary Feuchtenberger

Kevin and his family is their Christian faith. Though we haven't seen Kevin in many years, social media keeps us in touch with his family and his mother Wanda.

Beth was attractive and enjoyed the social part of school and was always happy being with many friends. Our home was the local hang out house with a front porch where people could gather, and a basketball goal beckoned numerous kids to cluster around back. I was happy to provide food to the many, mostly neighborhood boys, who happened by. Beth's brother, Eric, almost 5 years younger, also enjoyed that our home was the go to place. Todd, Brian and David visited often, as did many others.

Todd was a special friend who lived next door. He was a well behaved, kind person. Beth often joined him for breakfast prepared by his Mom, a kind woman and a fabulous cook! We were devastated when he collapsed just after Christmas on the basketball court of Princeton Junior High. Those undiagnosed heart problems bring unspeakable grief when one passes so young and unexpectedly. We lost two other young friends within a year. Jason had spent the day with Eric and then went to fish. He was only eleven years old and was struck by a car as he climbed the hill above the creek to go home. Beth's good friend Sean died in a car accident. A favorite memory of Sean is of him stopping by for Doug to assist with his tie on his way for graduation photos. He was full of smiles and happiness. I still feel sadness for the families and friends of those lost. Jenny is the bestie now, and we love knowing that she is part of us. We are also thankful for Timmy's family with his Mom Jan and sisters Pam, Kim and Teresa. Family is key!

One instance of Beth's young teenage days lingers in our "remember when" bank. I began looking for Beth and 3 or 4 others who were visiting in the back yard just at dusk. She was nowhere to be found. I yelled and yelled and began walking through the neighborhood. Suddenly, she appeared back at home. I caught just the whiff of a familiar smell and was certain that she had consumed some alcohol. I marched her inside, despite her denials, and berated her poor choices. She continued in denial, finally saying, "Oh Mom, you are so Superspicious!" Then, I was sure of her consumption, as she tried to reason with me that Superspicious was really a word. Of course, she had meant that I was suspicious. And I was! Oops, and I now find that Superspicious is a word, not in Webster's, but in the Urban Dictionary!

We were an average, middle class family living in an old two story brick house in downtown Princeton, WV. We still live there. Princeton is a small town where many people stay friends for life. Unfortunately, we are known for one horrible event in the 1980's. I never knew the person, but he decided to take a swim in the water tower on the hill in the Ingleside area. What he didn't realize was that, while you could climb a ladder to get in, there was no way out. It took some time to determine the cause of smelly water complaints, but finally, body parts were discovered in the tower. Eventually that tower was removed and memories of the tragedy faded. Princeton is also known as the home of Bob Denver, aka Gilligan and his wife Dreama and their son. She has written a gut wrenching book of their difficulties in raising a disabled child. The book, Gilligan's Dreams: The Other Side of the Island, will enlighten you to the hardships that some parents endure. Bob died in 2005. Dreama continues to operate Little Buddy Radio, a nonprofit station, to assist with the lives of special needs people.

My first teaching experience was at Spanishburg School. I took a job teaching summer school as soon as I graduated college. Then, in the fall, I began teaching at Oakvale School. Both were difficult in the beginning, because I was 21 and teaching 15 and 16 year olds. Now, I have great memories of those years and the special people that I had the honor of teaching and knowing through the years. The remaining 26 years of my career were at Princeton Junior/Middle School. My first year there, I took a personal day to pick Doug up at the hospital after his knee surgery. While signing him out, news of a fire became widespread. The Junior High was burning! Every person exited the building unharmed! We were praising God for that miracle. My husband Doug was a hard working coal miner who wasn't at home a lot due to long work hours and a lengthy drive, but he loved his family and provided for them well. His damaged knee was possibly the result of moving from place to place inside the mines on his knees. He told me that I could experience what his work day was like if I would just crawl under the dining room table all day! Yet, he did like his job!

When puberty hit Beth, it hit hard, and she dated several boys before Hank came into the picture. I really didn't know much about him, because he wasn't in school. She began seeing him at a difficult time in my and her Dad's life, and my keen powers of observation were not there. I think that I just assumed that she was working or with friends, when she was building a major relationship. My husband, Doug, had recently ended his coal mining business in Kentucky, and along with that came major debt and money problems that caused marriage stress. Also, my mother was very ill and passed away during this time. Regardless of the reasons, Beth was in love with the wrong person.

Hank told us that he had grown up in a household with horrible abuse. He had questionable morals, learning disabilities and though, only 15, was not attending school. Probably because of his age and inadequate education, he did not have a job and still lived with his family, including several brothers and sisters and both parents. He got into trouble often and had confrontations with many people. This information was not shared with me until much later. I just received little tidbits that they were dating. I learned that Hank's family was in need of food and household items by examining Beth's checkbook in secrecy. I found several checks written to grocery stores and realized that she wanted to assist them. The money spent amounted to several hundred dollars in a few weeks time. I had allowed her to keep her work money to spend on clothing and her needs. I fully trusted her, and guess that I found it was acceptable to buy food for needy people.

As we began to be concerned for our daughter and for our relationship...where did we turn? It is sad, but, so true of many, that we wait for a shattering event to give God some of our time. So, we found a church that we liked and attended until the pastor left for a new ministry. Then, we visited other churches, but did not attend on a regular basis. It is easy to break that habit. I now emphasize the importance of church! There are tremendous rewards!

Beth graduated high school in June of 1990 and began studies at a nearby college. We knew by now that Hank and Beth were in a binding relationship, and that he was known for breaking the law. His main problem was being defiant, fighting and hurting people. He had won boxing awards as a young teenager and now used people as punching bags. He was quick to anger and threatened people with bodily harm if they didn't comply with his wishes. He seemed to love being a bully and was nicknamed "Hank the Tank." Certainly, he was not a tank. He was trim and small in stature, but had amazing prowess, and his demeanor frightened most everyone.

By the second semester of college, Beth told me that she was ending their relationship. I was overjoyed! However, it was not that easy. And, things soon became worse instead of better. In April of 1991 she came to me with a pregnancy test kit. We did pray for negative results, but that was not the case. As I had come to know Hank better, I developed an extreme dislike for him, and was sure that I could never care for a baby fathered by him, but Beth and I both felt that the only choice was to have this baby and raise it with love and God's help.

Beth resumed her relationship with Hank and on December 13, 1991 (yes, it was Friday the 13) Hank Russell Jr. was born. He was a beautiful baby with lots of dark brown hair and brown eyes. He was our first grandchild! Immediately, I loved the grand baby that I had never wanted! The decision was made to call him by his middle name, Russell, to avoid confusion with his dad's name.

Beth decided that she would take the spring semester off from college, since a new baby is very time consuming. Hank escalated his control mechanism with Russell's birth and would direct Beth when and where to pick him up to visit with his baby and spend time with his family. Hank did not have a car, so Beth was the chauffeur. After Russell's birth, I became their chauffeur for a few weeks. At one point, Hank threatened me until I shook uncontrollably for the entire night! He told me, in no uncertain terms, that his baby would go with him in the middle of a cold winter night and NO ONE could keep him from access to his son!!!!! He WOULD have him whenever he wished and wherever he wished, and anyone who thought otherwise would suffer a severe penalty. Russell was his son! Russell was his son! Russell was his son!!! I had never been so afraid in my entire life.

I had picked Hank, Beth and Russell up past midnight at their friend's house when Russell was only 2 weeks old. My assumption was that I would take Hank to his house and Beth and Russell to ours. But, that was not to be. Hank insisted that Beth get baby gear together and stay at his family trailer. I nicely said that I thought it would be best if Beth could stay at our home with Russell for the night, since weather conditions were treacherous, and she could visit with Hank tomorrow. Unbelievable hell broke loose! He screamed and screamed and screamed at me from the top of his lungs over and over and over! At no point in my lifetime had I ever experienced such terror! I became afraid for my life and my daughter's life and safety. I knew, without a doubt, that if I told Doug of Hank's outbursts he would kill Hank, so I did not tell. Doug would be in jail and things would be even worse, so I left Doug sleeping, and he was not aware of the trauma that we had faced.

That confrontation took me much closer to God. Many prayers were sent out and many were answered. I am closer to God because of horrible events in my life. Since that night, Beth did begin to voice her concerns over Hank's behavior and filled me in on harrowing past events. She told of how, prior to her pregnancy, he had her drive him down one of those narrow, curving, mountain country roads that WV is known for. It is a dark black night without street lights, and he thinks that it is fun to apply his foot to the gas pedal with her steering the car. She was terrified, and had finally gotten the car stopped, jumped out and ran to a nearby house, only to have him grab her hair and drag her back. A frightened older couple had come to their front door in nightclothes, and could offer no help as they looked on, in dismay. Constantly she was told that he would burn her house or kill her parents and brother if she ever tried to leave him. Believe me, she was afraid! There was just so much that she had shielded us from.

With Russell's birth, we found it was best to make a few plans to accommodate Hank. We believed that Hank loved Russell very much, and because he wanted time with him, we finally allowed him to stay the night in our home. This lessened his requirement for Beth to take Russell out at all hours. We had a downstairs bedroom with twin beds and a crib, and this became somewhat of a refuge for Beth and Russell. Hank did not move in, but did stay several nights. And, at this time, Beth still professed to care for Hank. Doug and I, and Eric slept upstairs. It was very hard to accept this arrangement, but people make allowances under duress, and it eased tensions for a short time.

Now, I was raised in what we called a Holy Roller church. If you attended a church like mine, you know that you can take your problems to The Lord. It was difficult growing up with my mother and her religious beliefs. Part of the problem was her mental illness intermingled with religion. When I was nine years old, her mental health necessitated a short stay in Weston Mental Hospital. She was very strict with what she considered appropriate behavior. I was going to hell if I went to a movie. I was going to hell if I cut my hair. I was going to hell if I wore lipstick. I was going to hell if I told a lie. I felt, that no matter what I did, I was going to hell! I could never be good enough.

However, she did instill a strong knowledge in me that through Christ all things are possible. So, I knew where to turn when dealing with Hank's rages became intolerable. Actually, Hank had enough knowledge of the Lord to know he best leave us alone. I called my Mom's sister who was a wonderful prayer warrior, and she called the 700 Club and her church family. I called several local churches. Prayer was requested from every venue and, once again, I knew that it was time, actually past time, to find a church to attend.

We had neighbors, Sonny and Harriet, who had attended First Christian Church with their sons John and Eric, and I had childhood and family friends there. Earl and Peggy, who I had babysat for years ago, were members with their children Ellen and Steve. Doug saw Bobby that he had worked with in the coal mines, and that increased his comfort level. We were happy to be attending church with the family and found that the weeks that we went to church were always better than when we didn't. Twenty three years later, we still feel that way. We are there because of Russell and our love of God!

Yet, the devil, in the form of Hank, continued to wage war against us. Finally, Beth became fearful for her baby. Hank was making demands that caused her to worry for Russell and for herself. Late one night when Hank insisted that she come for him with Russell, she said NO! The turmoil began! He threatened our lives and said that he would come, and he WOULD have his child, and he would do whatever it took to get him. NO ONE could keep him from his child! The city police were called and responded immediately. Thank you Lord! And, thank you city police for your quick arrival! I am one person who appreciates you, although we have had you visit our home for other unhappy reasons.

We were advised to get a restraining order, so Doug went with Beth to the magistrate court, and Eric and I stayed at home with Russell, fearfully waiting for their return. Soon after they left, we heard frightening noises and began to feel very afraid. Things are being thrown at an upstairs window, and we are certain that Hank is on the roof about to break in. One level of our roof has access to Eric's bedroom window. We know that Hank will hurt us and take his baby! The horror is unreal! It is hard to imagine that so much evil can come into our lives.

I am in my own home with my 14 year old son and 5 month old grandson feeling helpless. What if Hank crashes in the window? I visualize glass breaking as he comes in with weapons and fists to harm, possibly to kill us. My heart is beating rapidly, and I am shaking. The police are again called, and several cars with flashing lights arrive quickly. Two young men are found in our yard throwing rocks at Eric's bedroom window. How is it, that, on the very worst night imaginable, two of Eric's good, neighborhood friends have come by to try to coax Eric to sneak out for some teenage fun?

Boy, did they get a huge surprise!!! They were shaken down and carted off to jail. One received a huge goose egg above his eye as a lesson. Eric says that, unfortunately, this disaster ended their friendship, though not our fault. It is very funny in retrospect, but will always be remembered as one of the worst circumstances of our lives. Eric's friends had totally picked the wrong night, and our fear was unfounded for the moment. Doug and Beth returned with the court order, and a sleepless night slowly passed.

Beth realized that she needed to get an education to support her baby by herself, so she returned to college that summer, and I kept Russell while she went to school. I was now needed to protect him and couldn't return to my job at the junior high to finalize year end paper work. This trauma was keeping me behind locked doors with my precious grandson.

Teacher friends were amazing, and I thank Sandy, Rhonda and others, again for their kindness of completing my schoolwork so many years ago. Sandy is a favorite friend who invited me to accompany her to Mountain Lake back in the 1980's. Because it was about an hour's drive, I decided that I was too busy to join her. She said that they were filming some little movie and that her daughter Stacey was chosen from local dancers for a bit role. Whew! I totally missed that one, as Dirty Dancing became the hit movie of the century! I worked with great people including Kay, Jan, Pat, Ginger, Allen, Jeff and principals, Ted and Joe. We always enjoyed each others' company and socializing. Ginger told a funny story that still makes me laugh when I think of it. A child had missed school and his parent sent a note that said "Johnny missed school yesterday because he wasn't in the car when we left!" I could definitely relate to that!

As the school year ended, I had a terrible summer for sure! I had to watch each direction when I left the house and hurry to the car with Russell. We were always fearful that Hank was lurking around every corner, and his Mother was also an issue. Beth told me that Hank's Mom had once stabbed a person, and that if I ever saw her, I should quickly turn in the opposite direction, because she most likely would try to hurt me. That dreaded, scary day did come!

Mary Feuchtenberger

I could barely believe it when Hank and his mom drove up in front of our home, casually walked up the sidewalk and knocked on our door. I am in a dilemma over what to do. I was home alone with Russell and felt completely terrorized. I was watching the window, as I had gotten in the habit of doing, and immediately rushed to the phone and called the police. This was before cell phones, so getting to a phone was a major priority. We were prepared with a gun on the fireplace mantle. Though trembling, I grabbed it, tried to remember how to use it and thought that I might have to shoot Hank. Actually, I wanted to and had to talk myself out of it. Fear brings uncharacteristic behavior and as a child of God, I knew that would be wrong. I had never fired a gun, but I felt that I could, if necessary, to protect myself and Russell. I yelled through the door to Hank and his Mom, and they suggested, innocently, that they only wanted to visit with Russell. Yeah right! I responded that we had the restraining order, and he could not visit, so they left.

I don't know what other plans they had, but the police arrived shortly thereafter, and located and took Hank to jail for violating the order. As the 60 days of the court restriction passed without problems, arrangements were made with the Department of Human Services for Hank to have supervised visitation with Russell. Kira, now our neighbor, provided that service. It seems that parental rights are protected even in the worst of circumstances. But, Hank did well and was awarded unsupervised visitation after several months. Unbelievably, he and Beth reached a point where they could talk, and Russell was allowed to stay with Hank and his family for short periods. Their family definitely loved Russell and enjoyed keeping him, and Russell never hesitated to go with them. Prayer allows amazing things, and we know that GOD delivered this transition.

In remembering all the drama and worry that we went through, I realize, now, how unnecessary it was. The hymn, "What a Friend We Have in Jesus," written in 1855 by Joseph Scriven, says it all and reminds us of how to live in peace.

What a friend we have in Jesus, All our sins and grief to bear, what a privilege to carry everything to God in prayer! Oh, what peace we often forfeit, Oh, what needless pain we bear, all because we do not carry, everything to God in prayer! Have we trials and temptations Is there trouble anywhere? We should never be discouraged. Take it to the Lord in prayer.

What mighty words written so long ago to offer comfort. We sang that hymn this past Sunday. Church attendance has wonderful benefits! Mark 11:24. (NIV) **"Therefore I tell you, whatever you ask for in prayer, believe that you have received it, and it will be yours."**

In looking at job choices that might pay well and not require a 4 year degree, x-ray technician seemed a good choice. Beth and I discussed the pros and cons. She wasn't a real science person, but we thought she could x-ray people with broken bones and wouldn't have to deal with much of the blood and guts of hospital drama. Little did we know!!! Early in her internship I received a phone call from her in tears. A baby, close in age to Russell, had been brought in with head injuries. His parent had shaken him until he hemorrhaged and later died. Beth just didn't think that she could continue in this field. Within a few nights, I received a phone call from Beth. It was almost a repeat of the other call, and this baby also died. It was horrible for Beth to deal with at age 20 with a young baby at home herself. Another difficult procedure that we had not thought of was the x-raying of bones during surgery. Beth found herself getting dizzy, up chucking and passing out after being called in to x-ray during shoulder surgery. My sweet daughter was led into the wrong profession by her mom who was...well, now you know, a science teacher.

She survived her training at the local hospital and graduated in 2 years. She quickly found a job with Dr. Craft and learned to multitask. She even became proficient at taking blood. Seeing blood and having it taken as a child was a major phobia for her, and now she was on the performing end. Her son will never know the life challenges and sacrifices that she faced to support him. The doctor's office job was a good experience overall, and the doctor was a wonderful person. It was sad when he closed his business, and Beth went to work at the local hospital. First, she worked in general x-ray, but found that sonography better suited her. She feels fortunate to have Dr. Ahmed as her mentor. The hospital offered training, and she still has continuing education classes and works solely with sonograms and is the department head.

Side note: It is sad how quickly I can have doubts, and I fear that prayer will not work. Yet, I do know that prayer is the answer, but I am horrified to think that I may have to deal with another family member using drugs. My granddaughter will be 17 in a few days. She is a defiant teenager and is now smoking and drinking at times. Her grades are not good, and she doesn't want to be told how to behave. There seems to be a possibility of drug use with some of her postings. Is it just for attention or part of her life? I am sick with worry, but wait...here I am, telling the world to turn it over to The Lord. Believe me! I do know how hard that is to do.

Doug and I are very worried. However...we are not to worry. For whatever we ask in His name we shall receive, if only we believe. I love The Lord with all of my heart, yet my faith fails me at times. The devil creeps in. My thoughts show terrible doubt, and I think of the Bible, "**Oh you of little faith.**" In Mark 11:22-24 CEV Jesus told his disciples: **"Have faith in God. If you have faith in God and don't doubt, you can tell that mountain to get up and jump into the sea, and it will. Everything you ask in prayer will be yours, if you only have faith."** I know not to worry, yet I am thinking different scenarios. She may be on hard drugs... pills???? I tell my daughter, Beth, that I am ready to go to heaven. I do not want to deal with another loved one on drugs. This is the same precious grand daughter who was our pride and joy for many years. I think of a funny time that I took her to the grocery store when she was 3 or 4 years old. We strolled to the lobster tank, and I selected a couple for our meal. Immediately, she voiced her concern, "Granny, I don't want any Monster for dinner."

We read Bible stories often and went to her baptism at age eight when she chose the Lord as her savior! I stress and do not sleep. Yes, I am being disobedient to God with my worry. I rearm myself with prayer and Bible study. I think how ashamed that I am to doubt. We know the solution. Sunday, in church, Doug and I go forward and ask the elders to gather around us and pray. Doug says that immediately he feels uplifted.

We know that she will return to a drug free life. Her Mamaw, Donna, faithfully took her to church each Sunday as a child, and she knows God! She is our second grandchild and our son, Eric, is her Father. Like Beth, Eric became a parent at age 19. He dated our granddaughter's Mom for over a year, and she became pregnant. Our granddaughter was a beautiful baby and easy to care for. Her parents were happy for us to keep her, and we got into the habit of having her overnight most Saturdays. Then, she began to spend many days and nights with us to the point that she was with us more than with her parents. And, Eric and her mom divorced and both remarried.

We spoiled our granddaughter, and our home was her choice, until she became a defiant teenager, and we gave her back. To think of her on drugs was more than I could bear. God did answer immediately. She had not been having much contact with us. Basically, we were her taxi, but she had curtailed visits with us as her interest in worldly ventures increased. But, after our prayer in church, she began to stay at our home for several hours after school most weekdays. And, we began to talk. And, yes, she had been smoking pot and joined with kids who did even more. Suddenly, she had a choking experience with a legal synthetic drug and felt she should stop its' use. She now believes this event will keep her from future drug use and says that she would always recommend a drug free life. We praise God! There is still much difficulty and drama in her life, but I have let it go.

God is in charge! There are so many young people who need prayer warriors. I do pray for her and those around her. I try to be specific. I ask that our granddaughter and her peers obey God and live a Christian life. I ask that they be polite to others, and that they respect their parents and teachers. I pray for good grades and appropriate dress and resistances to drugs and alcohol. And, I ask for blessings. Please God guide my children and grandchildren and all those around each of us. Please help each of us to have the right values. There is so much evil. And, Lord, take away my evil. Mine is there and may not as visible as some, but it is there every day.

Even my 97 year old uncle says that evil waits on him to do wrong. And I think, surely that cannot be since he is such a God fearing man. Every event at his church is certain to be blessed with his attendance. When I have asked him to pray for Russell, he readily agrees and says that he spends very much time on his knees. I know that he can barely walk and has many aches and pains, but he honors God by turning his countenance to him. The Bible James 4:8: **Move close to God and he will move close to you**. He is so good, and He is our parent who loves us and wants only the best for us.

Will you accept the best? In the Message version of the Bible, He says he will throw us a party. Imagine the streets of Gold when we get to heaven. This earthly existence is just a speck in our life. Can you give the time and honor to Him? If so, your life will be enriched beyond your belief.

Notes 2
(Back to Russell)

I keep journals, but sometimes I do not write in one for weeks, months and even years. I have searched them for information concerning Russell. Old emails remind me of difficult circumstances with Russell. Friends and family members have shared a few of their memories, also.

I will say that as a baby, Russell brought a lot of joy to our home. Doug and I celebrated twenty years of marriage on December 26, 1991, just two weeks after his birth. We had a party in our home and delighted in showing off our new grandson to guests. We received wonderful comments. "Isn't he the most beautiful baby? Look at all that hair. His eyes are so alert and very dark brown. Wow, he is very strong. Look, he smiled!" Yes, we have an addition to the household and welcome all the baby praises. There is nothing that compares to the joy this newborn brings to us, his grandparents. Things were very festive. I bragged that Beth had the most handsome baby and that our Christmas tree decorated with angels and hearts was beyond compare in all of Princeton! The evening was jubilant, yet circumstances change, and the real world comes crashing down. The next night is the one in which Hank insisted on taking Beth and Russell out and threatened me, so that I shook and trembled for hours.

We did have many hard times, but also many good. Often, Russell would fall asleep with me holding him. It is a wonderful feeling to have him in my arms. The first smile and every one after it fills me with intense love. I grit my teeth a lot. It is a strong love reflex. Then, there are the first words and efforts to crawl and to walk. But, this is also the time we acquired a restraining order for Hank. Anyone familiar with him feels that Hank will try to take Russell and cause us bodily harm, so we spend many restless nights. However, Russell is a good baby and enriches our lives. Later, and on much better terms, I talked with Hank about his threats. His response was surprising. He said that he was afraid of God and knew our Christian beliefs and felt that he should not harass us.

For part of his life, Hank had lived with a Christian family. I'm not sure of the reason, but they were family friends and offered to keep him, and he learned about God from them. The woman, Erma Jean, is now, and has been for many years, a pastor of a local Pentecostal church. Beth attended this church with and without Hank. After all the turmoil it is hard to believe that Hank and Beth were baptized together by this pastor, on October 3, 1992, when Russell was 10 months old. I think of the old folk hymn "Down to the River to Pray" since the river was where they were baptized.

"As I went down in the river to pray studying about that good old way and who shall wear the starry crown. Good Lord, show me the way! O sister let's go down, let's go down, come on down, O sisters, let's go down, Down in the river to pray." Beth and Hank were no longer romantically involved and were hardly friends, but both were Russell's parents. God provided answers to so many prayers.

By November of 1992, Russell is beginning to walk. He loves watching Barney, the purple dinosaur and playing with Barney toys. His room is decorated with purple sheets and curtains and every Barney item imaginable. He was like SpongeBob is today. Another favorite toy is a small indoor basketball goal. He can make amazing shots by age one. His athletic ability is very evident. We love having his first Christmas in our home. A baby brings much pleasure to the holidays and to every day.

Russell goes to daycare while Beth attends college, and I work. Sometimes his Dad or Dad's family would keep him. They love him very much. Doug's Mom and Dad occasionally ask to keep him. They were in their early seventies with some free time and what can be better than a baby? Russell has many people who love him. We attend church on a regular basis and teach Russell about God. Bible stories are read and explained to him, and prayer is part of his night time ritual.

Hank visits our home when Russell is 16 months old. He asks us to forgive him. In the Bible Matthew 18:21 (NKJV) **"Then Peter came to Him and said "Lord, how often shall my brother sin against me and I forgive him? Up to seven times?" Jesus said to him, "I do not say to you, up to seven times, but up to seventy times seven."**

I feel that I am pretty good at forgiving, but it can be hard, extremely hard. As I was reading The Purpose Driven Life there came a point in the book that urged people to ask forgiveness of anyone they thought might feel wronged by them. I did have one person who instantly came to mind. I tried to let it go and forget that I should ask forgiveness. I struggled with it and didn't want to back track. Yet, as I continued to read, Rick Warren again urged people to do that. With dread, it needed to be done. I wrote the letter requesting forgiveness, satisfied that it was the right thing to do. The person wrote back that I was forgiven. The Bible questions, if we cannot forgive, how can our Father in heaven forgive us?

In June of 1993, Beth begins dating. She has waited over a year, for fear of animosity from Hank. I am keeping Russell more while school is out for the summer, and it can be difficult. He has tremendous energy, and it is hard for him to understand the meaning of the word NO! The terrible twos have arrived, just a little early. By the time that Russell is three, Beth has gotten married, and her husband manages having a young child okay. Russell does well in school and excels in athletics. Basketball is a favorite game, but he enjoys most any sport. He rides a bike without training wheels sooner than anyone at day care and loves motorcycles, four wheelers, trucks and cars...

Mary Feuchtenberger

After seven years of marriage, Beth is unhappy and divorces. Russell is very hurt and misses his stepdad and never has any contact with him. He wonders why and asks me, but I have no answers. He could have visited with him, since we all live in the same area. He never asks to see Russell.

In a couple of years, Beth remarries. We all like Timmy and his young daughter, but Russell has problems with rules from his parents and, in early adolescence, becomes a very difficult child. He was diagnosed as ADHD in second grade. Even his preschool teacher suggested that he might need medication. Beth took him for counseling on a regular basis, and he was prescribed medicine for attention deficit hyperactivity disorder. Most of the time we found the medicine helped. Without it, he was very active and difficult to calm down. He could not concentrate.

Unfortunately, he also had oppositional defiance disorder. Our family members became trained in positive reinforcement. Much of the time it helped, but with increasing age came increasing difficulties. It is hard to maintain a child with these problems. Russell could not help much of his behavior, although some people thought that he could. It is difficult for an ADHD child to stay focused and on task.

After several suspensions and behavior write-ups in eighth grade, it was decided to remove him from that school. Our county has a highly rated church school, and he was enrolled there for his last semester of middle school. While he still had difficulty, his grades and conduct did improve. One problem developed when I became his taxi to and from school. It tied up my time every day. I was pleased for him to enroll in regular high school his freshman year.

Again, he had difficulties and was a discipline problem at home. Much of his defiance focused on his Mom and stepdad. They pretty much had their hands full working and caring for their two daughters ages one and two, and keeping Timmy's 13 year old daughter much of the time. Hoping to diffuse the situation, our son Eric offered Russell the opportunity to live with him, and his wife Shawna agreed.

Russell was happy staying in their home and things went well... for a while. He completed ninth grade, but could not conform to

Groundhog Day in West Virginia

school rules and requirements the next year. Finally, the school counselor recommended the alternative school. There, attendance is in the evenings with much of the work done on computers. It was a wonderful solution…for a while.

But, he would not continue with this program to completion and it was decided that at age 16, he would attend GED school. His classes would be during the day with some flexibility in attendance. He had quit his ADHD medicine and doctor visits at age 15 against his Mom's wishes. This hindered his success in school. Since we live near this school and I had retired from teaching, we allowed him to live with us. He could walk to school or I would take him. However, he suffered a scary event walking to a friend's house one morning, and this diminished his comfort in walking alone in Princeton.

On the walk to the friend's house, he was stopped by three young thugs in a car. They knew that he was "Hank the Tank's" son and wanted to fight him. Of course, it was three against one, and they thought that was fair. When he later recounted the event to me, it was heart wrenching. They had driven their car right onto the curb and cornered him. Upon being punched, he remembers that he went into a rage. The two boys who got out of the car were severely beaten by Russell, until a stranger came along, stopped the fight and drove him to his friend's house. This was a problem that his Dad Hank had and complained about. Once you are known for being good at fighting, or as he had been with boxing, people want to test you. It is hard to get away. One good solution may be to move to another city. Hank was feared in our area. When Russell was two, Hank was found guilty of beating three men in a bar. He was confined to prison for several years. There had been numerous times that he hurt people and had not been prosecuted. It was good that the law finally caught him, and he even agreed with that.

I had never visited anyone in jail, but I did visit Hank. He was in prison a little over 40 miles from where we live. I had spent the day antiquing in a town several miles from there. On my way home, I passed Southern Regional Jail. Oddly enough, I decided that I should stop and visit Hank. It certainly was not planned. Today, I know that appointments are required for visits. If that was the case then, I was never told. A former student, with whom I had a good relationship, was in control at the check-in desk. Apparently, I had arrived at the perfect time. God does provide even before we know the need! I remember feeling some embarrassment at knowing an inmate, but other people were there for the same reason. The former student was very nice and made the visitation process easy. Thank you God!

Hank was surprised, but glad to see me. I told him that I felt compelled to stop and tell him that Russell was doing well. This was a short time after Beth's marriage, and I knew that the idea of another man with his son bothered Hank. I assured him that his son was happy. He emphasized his love for Russell, and said that he worried about a stepfather hurting Russell. Hank said that he had been horribly abused and this made him fearful for his son. I assured him that Beth would never tolerate abuse and that her husband was good to Russell.

Hank confided to me that jail was actually where he needed to be. He said that he had been using drugs, one of which was cocaine, and that his life was a mess. His incarceration was a good thing! He and I talked about The Lord, and he would always say that he wanted to be closer to Him, but it was very hard. The people that he surrounded himself with made his choices difficult, and he did not have a good family support system. Still, there were times that he prayed. Hank made a point, whenever I talked with him, to say that he loved Beth and that he loved Doug and me. He knew that he had wronged us and said that he would not bother us again, and he was glad for Beth to be married.

Russell did visit his Dad occasionally when he was in jail. Hank's mom would take him with several other family members. He was happy to go and spend time with them. When Hank was released from jail, he saw Russell on a regular basis for a year or so. Even Hank had trouble disciplining him. A few times, Russell would call me to come and get him early and I did. Now, I believe, Russell just refused to comply with his Dad's wishes, and rather than face punishment, he called me. I was too quick to rescue him.

Notes 3
(Hank)

As Russell got older, he didn't see his Dad often. Hank began living with a woman, who, I feel, that he loved. Hopefully, he did not terrorize her as he did Russell's Mom, but most likely, she experienced many frightening moments. I had occasion to meet with them, because I volunteered to take Russell to their home for paternal visits. Hank, at that time, had 3 children with Anna, and, although they were much younger than he was, Russell enjoyed being with them and loved his siblings. I never really knew how Hank provided for his family, but I imagine it was a struggle. So many people just do without things that others take for granted. The WV Department of Human Services, what we call Welfare, probably gave food stamps and some money. Beth did not receive child support. I think that she received $50.00 one or two times when Hank had a job, and his check was garnished. Hank's wife worked for a year or so as a waitress, and, possibly, Hank kept their children. He didn't seem to have a work ethic.

We never heard much good about him. He was probably on drugs. It is horrible to even think of what his little kids faced. Many children in southern WV and other drug infested areas have a sad and dangerous life without parents to watch after them. Poverty takes its' toll. I recently saw Jennifer Garner on a PBS documentary. She is a proud WV native and is working with a program to help children through education. Accolades to her and many others who are trying to make a difference! I grew up with very little, and my education was the key to much of my success in life. My husband's upbringing was on the other end of the spectrum.

Doug's family was well to do, but, conservative with their income. God, education and work were major values in his home as well as mine. Doug completed his education at Fork Union Military Academy. His brothers John and Rollie are law school graduates. His brother Mark graduated high school, but health issues kept him from finishing college. His sister Betse attended high school at National Cathedral in Washington DC.

Betse told me of sitting next to a fellow student and discussing their fathers' work. The girl asked Betse, "What does your Father do?" Betse replied, "He works in a bakery. What does your Father do?" The girl answered, "He is president. Betse said, "Oh, my father is president, too, of Betsy Ross Bakery. What is your Father President of?" The girl, Luci Baines Johnson, answered, "The United States!" I have seldom laughed so much! Betse completed her education at Hollins University in Virginia and is a fabulous writer who worked in advertising.

Another major difference in our upbringing became evident when I went to see the movie "The Help" with Betse and Rollie. As they watched, they were often in tears as they remembered "the help" in their home. They lived in a huge home with their parents and a total of five children. Their Mother taught school while their Dad worked at the bakery. The children were fortunate to have kind, educated black ladies care for their home and prepare food and also to mentor them. I think of the time that Doug told his Mom that we were expecting our first child. She was excited and went to tell Frances, who was "the help." She replied, "Oh, I already know. Douglas told me as soon as he came in the house!" The love they felt for these women was obvious as we left the movie and discussed earlier times.

Often, in my home, my grandmother was "the help." Many times we were in need of bare necessities, and she would work taking care of an elderly lady in poor health. While my grandmother was also elderly, she arose to the occasion and provided some income. Though our monetary statuses were opposites, my husband and I share similar values and both know that God is in control.

Now, life with our family takes unexpected turns! In August of 2006, I was awakened from my deep sleep by the ringing of the phone. Those calls in the middle of the night generally are not good news, and this one was unimaginable. It was Beth, calling to inform me that Hank had been murdered! His family had called for her to bring Russell, then 14, to the hospital. It was their feeling that he should be with them while they gathered in Hank's dying moments. As a family, they generally bonded closely in times of hardships. We heard that there was a lot of hospital drama, but really do not know. Emotions were probably raging with grief, hurt and talk of revenge. Beth refused to awaken Russell and place her young son in that turmoil. She chose to let him sleep until morning before delivering the startling news.

Russell had not been visiting with his Dad often, and that possibly helped him deal with the loss. However, a few years later, he turned his Dad into a martyr with a huge tattoo of boxing gloves on his back to give tribute to his Dad's passion. I still have Hank's boxing trophies in my attic. He didn't have a place for safe keeping them, and asked if they could be kept in our home for Russell someday. Russell loved his Dad, but they did not communicate regularly or spend much time together. When he got the tattoo, I found that to be a slap in his Mom's face, but some people have problems with their values.

I'm still not certain of why the man decided to kill Hank. Some say that he was Hank's sister's boyfriend and that there was a relationship problem that Hank felt the need to take care of. He would never step down if he felt threatened and would let everyone know not to mess with him or his family. Others have said that it was drug related. It is my understanding that they were arguing on the phone, and had agreed to meet in the parking lot of a small post office not far from our hometown. When Hank arrived, he got out of his car to speak with the person, and the man shot him in the chest.

nk was a sight to behold when he was angry, possibly reminiscent of the Incredible Hulk. He was not armed, but being known as a ferocious fighter, he surely was a tremendous threat to the man who pleaded guilty to manslaughter and was sentenced to 15 years in jail. I wonder how much of that time he will actually serve.

I have to admit that I cared for Hank. Yes, I did care for the man who threatened my life and tormented my daughter. Beth says that I don't know a lot of how he mistreated her, and that is probably best. The Lord says to forgive, and I have been able to do that. It is difficult to believe the hatred that I felt for him at one point in my life. Ephesians 4:31-32 NIV says to **"Get rid of all bitterness, rage and anger, brawling and slander, along with every form of malice. Be kind and compassionate to one another, forgiving each other, just as in Christ, God forgave you."** I feel very blessed that I was able to obey God.

Occasionally, Hank would call me to see how Russell was doing, and we would talk. Sometimes he came to our home to visit with Russell and play basketball around back. He was very polite and, after he lost his Mom, he seemed to have a need, at times, to seek advice from me. I wanted his salvation, and that was always a topic of conversation. Knowing The Lord was part of Hank's life, but he had tremendous problems with obedience. Many of us do. He wanted to do better, but met the devil at most every turn. I always told him to pray on his knees and ask The Lord to forgive him and to bless his life.

On the morning after Hank's death, Beth brought Russell to our home. She went on to work, and I kept him for the day. She had explained the circumstances of Hank's death and consoled Russell as much as she could. Russell wanted to go and see where it had happened. My feeling was that it is best to confront the situation and seek answers to any questions, so I accommodated him by driving the 10 miles or so to the little post office. We discussed the good and bad things in his Dad's life.

It was very sad to be with a child you love, looking at the spot where his father was murdered. Never in my life would I have ever thought of myself in this position. It was heartbreaking! We could see a large area of dried blood in the parking lot. We talked to several people who discussed what they knew about the confrontation. How does a young man take that in? I hoped that this trip would be beneficial and provide information about the details of the previous night. And, we prayed.

Next, we entered a little store across the street. The clerk working there said that she was with Hank just after he was shot. She was at work, heard the gunfire and left the store to find him bleeding. She said that she held him and prayed and felt that he acknowledged the prayer. He was picked up by ambulance and transported to our community hospital where he soon died. We discussed the fact that Hank did know The Lord and, hopefully, his last bit of energy was used to ask forgiveness.

Russell was pretty much what people call "the spitting image of his Dad." He immediately was pleased to reconnect with his Dad's family of many uncles, aunts and cousins coming to the visitation and funeral. It is obvious that he loves these people, and they love him, even though they seldom spend time together. They are family. While there, we learned that Russell's stepmom Anna is pregnant. She already has 2 sons and a daughter by Hank. The new baby is born several months later, and she gives him his dad's name...Hank Russell III. So now there are two---half brothers with the same name, but almost 15 years apart in age. The name seems an odd choice, but with her loss so recent, she wants this baby to have his father's name.

Our family vacation has been planned for months, and we leave for the beach just after Hank's burial. We enjoy being together and upon our return is the return to school. Russell manages to complete the school year, but not the next. He enrolls in the alternative night school after several suspensions from the regular high school. Later, I find that his daily pot smoking is a huge deterrent to his education. He fails to finish the Alternative school and the next year tries the GED school. He is successful with that...for a while. Probably his drug use is beginning to change from pot to pills. We don't have a clue. We just know that he is difficult to control. Later, he confides that this was the escalation of his pill use. Narcotic pill use is rampant in our area, and he becomes hooked. He gets a job at a local fast food place and is a good worker...for a while. Is that the story of his life? Good for a while?

He spends many nights with friends and is increasingly defiant. While GED seemed to be the solution, he doesn't want teachers and parents telling him what to do. He has developed many devious ways. Doug has noticed things missing from the garage and wonders if Russell has taken them. Doug is a tool guy...he loves his tools and knows how to use them. Our garage is home to many tool man's dreams. It makes me mad that he would think that our grandson has taken something. I feel sure that Doug has just misplaced that prized item. Unfortunately, I finally realize that Russell has done the same inside our home. When I am ready to take him to GED classes, we get in the car and oops, he has to go to the bathroom real fast or he forgot something. I give him my house key because we don't trust him with his own, and he goes in quickly to do whatever he said. He is back in a flash, returns my key and I take him to school, and tell him that I'm going shopping for a few hours.

One day I come back too soon. As I go in our home, I hear just the hint of something in the kitchen and find the back door closed, but unlocked. Since we have been concerned over missing possessions, I always double check our locks before leaving the house. We even keep doors locked when we are at home, because there are way too many suspicious people passing through the neighborhood. Russell is on the deck with friends and vehemently swears that he is just waiting out back for me to come home. The truth is that when he told me he needed to run back in to go to the bathroom, he was actually unlocking the back door. I didn't have a clue. Then, he and his friends could use our home as desired and take objects that might not be missed for a while. I often felt that I had misplaced something. At that time, I was an antique dealer and eBay seller, and it was difficult for me to keep track of the many items purchased for resale. But, now, I did realize, with so much hurt in my heart, that my grandson was a thief. Upon inspection, I found coins and jewelry were gone and countless other items.

I'm sure many people have been in the position of having a loved one steal from them. There is often much denial before acceptance of the fact. Drug use requires HUGE amounts of money. As Russell continued to be a terrible problem to us, he is charged with a crime. He was driving a borrowed 4 wheeler and accidentally ran into a car causing damage. He had no license or insurance. This did open the window of possibility for him to try a school that his Mom had been encouraging.

The court offered him a choice--school or jail. The National Guard has, in WV, a free residential 5-6 month program for students to live and take GED classes. I believe other states have similar schools that some people may be unaware of. I salute this school for their outstanding ability to formulate responsible behavior in students! However, Russell had no plan for attending such a school.

Notes 4
(Growing Up)

He pretty much laughed in our faces when we suggested it. He thought that he was invincible, and that if he shouted and cursed enough his will would be done. But we had a better idea. We wanted HIS will to be done, meaning our Lord Jesus Christ! Russell had brought us to Christ one more time. So many prayers were requested and answered! Thank you Lord!

Soon, in July of 2009 when Russell was 17, he was on his way to (MCA) Mountaineer Challenge Academy. This was the National Guard School that Beth's husband's nephew had attended and recommended. Russell said that he would try it for 2-3 weeks. Every person with a druggie in their household knows, I'm sure, how wonderful it is to be free of demands and problems even for a few hours! So we are elated! Oh, and by the way, we are praying. Possibly, we would be neglecting God if it were not for Russell. I feel certain that I never would have been on my knees so often if not for him.

Many of us get selfish with the time we give our Savior, not to even mention how stingy we get with our money. I can say that I am at a good point with the "money thing." I love to donate to our church and those in need. Much of my life, I felt that there was not any money to give. We spent every penny every month and then some. Credit card debt was an ongoing concern. Actually, I'm not sure what changed my mind about tithing. I just believe that as you come closer to God, your priorities change. How do you do that? Russell has definitely helped. He is here for a reason!

A quote attributed to Rick Warren states "your greatest ministry will likely come from your deepest pain" and that is true for me. I am putting that ministry on paper as I write this. And, I have also increased the time that I spend praying and reading the Bible and Christian books. The Purpose Driven Life by Rick Warren is one of my favorites. I've read it several times and plan to again. This book has sold millions of copies and has been long running on the best sellers list. I believe that it is one book that every person should read. It will guide you on ways to become closer to God and how to find your purpose on earth.

One of the first Bible quotes from the book is Proverbs 11:28 (MSG). **"A life devoted to things is a dead life, a stump; A God-shaped life is a flourishing tree." A verse I like to pair with it is John 15:5 (NIV) "I am the vine; you are the branches. If you remain in me and I in you, you will bear much fruit; apart from me you can do nothing."** Rick Warren encourages people to memorize scripture. My memorization skills are not the best, but I do print many of my favorite verses and read them often.

A good suggestion is to read the verses aloud to help with remembering them. Rick Warren also reminds us that church attendance is a priority. I have become more involved with church functions, but still have much room for improvement. As I have done these things, I am becoming a better Christian, which is my goal. I want that closer walk with God! Some words to the hymn, Just A Closer Walk With Thee follow:

I am weak but Thou art strong; Jesus, keep me from all wrong; I'll be satisfied as long, As I walk, let me walk close to Thee, Just a closer walk with Thee, Grant it Jesus is my plea, Daily walking close to Thee, Let it be, dear Lord, let it be.

Mary Feuchtenberger

I had taken early retirement from teaching at age 55. This made my income decrease by about 25% -30%. Now, does anyone ever have enough money? I didn't when I was working, so I knew that I would have to be careful with my retirement income, especially now that I had more time to shop. But, as I was becoming closer to God, I absolutely wanted to give him my money, and, so I did. And, I tried to give a little more than 10% because I owed him for many selfish years and because, with all my heart, I want to help our church.

Now you may have read this and heard it from pastors, you will reap what you sow or that God will return what you give and that is what happened. As Judy, a lady in our church has said, "you have a lot more to spend with 90% of your income than you do with 100% of your income." The Bible (NLT) Luke 6:38. **"Give and you will receive. Your gift will return to you in full---pressed down, shaken together to make room for more, running over, and poured into your lap. The amount you give will determine the amount you get back." The Lord loves a cheerful giver: 2 Corinthians 9:7 NIV. "Each man should give, not reluctantly or under compulsion, for God loves a cheerful giver."**

I never thought that would describe me, but it does! I want to return Gods gifts and to help other people. An astonishing side effect is that I have money left in my bank account every single month. And, it's not just a little bit left each month. I've tried to do the math a few times, and it really doesn't compute. My retirement income is less, my bills are actually more, with cost of living increases, and I am tithing regularly. Now, I have more money than when I was working and giving less to the church. But, the reason to tithe is not so you will have more. Tithe because you love God and want to help others.

Moving close to God requires your conscious decision. It is easy to be side tracked. Be sure to talk with the Lord each day and ask for his guidance. Read the Bible and Christian books. Always pray! Find a church that you like and attend regularly. Since my closer walk with God, I now know for certain that I am going to heaven! I am looking forward to it! According to 1 Corinthians 2:9, **No eye has seen, no ear has heard, and no mind has imagined what God**

has prepared for those who love Him. Can you envision being in heaven? What a joyous day that will be. When we all see Jesus... Do you know where you are going? Can you improve your life with God? Are you willing to help your loved one escape the evil in their life by asking God for help? Move close to God. You will find the peace that surpasses understanding.

In June of 2009 we began receiving one kind of peace when Russell started attending the National Guard School. They require drug testing and respect. They teach life skills and perform community service acts on a regular basis. They hold students to strict rules while they work on their GED. Again, I cannot recommend this school enough. It is a blessing to have Russell out of our hair, so to speak... for a while. He is not even allowed to visit for a month or so. Too bad, so sad...not! I do not miss him.

Actually, we finally have peace of mind for the first time in several years. We have always been terrible enablers, and if he made a request we often fulfilled it. He used reasonable excuses. He required money for a new pair of shoes, a friend was taking him somewhere and needed gas, he had a date, he was hungry and on and on and on and on. Very often he needed us to drive him somewhere. This "man" required much of our time and our income. I asked him recently where he got the money when he was using pot in Jr. High. He said "from you Granny or from Pappy."

We wanted to be sure that he had lunch money or whatever he said he needed. And, on a good note, he would work for money. Russell could do a job easily, quickly and to our satisfaction. He always seemed happy to help us. Little did we know, until much later, that he was spending on an increasingly bad habit that became an addiction. Many parents and grandparents today want to be sure that their kids have the best of the best. God forbid that they may not have a brand name tennis shoe or the finest phone. Yes, I was guilty.

It is a world different from the one in which I grew up. Kids are mean to each other and make fun of you, if you don't have the "right stuff." I grew up with zero of what kids call the right stuff. Therefore, again, I plead guilty to providing way too much for

Mary Feuchtenberger

Russell. It is heartbreaking to realize the amount of drugs that were purchased with grandparent money. I was trying to provide the best and, instead, fostered the worst.

Now, as an adult, I believe that being poor was the best way to be raised. I did not feel entitled. I never had doubt, that, when I was growing up, we did not have money for clothes, for food, for school supplies, for hardly anything. I was lucky to get one Christmas gift. I knew not to ask, and just accepted that I would do without.

Honestly, we did eat beans every day, but one side effect of being poor was the tremendous bounties of food directly from God. Living two blocks from the courthouse on a very small area of land, we had apple, pear and walnut trees. Raspberries and blackberries grew in abundance in our back yard, as did grapes. The presence of these fruits meant that a daily treat of homemade jelly and jams was available. Often, I savored huge glasses full of homemade grape juice. Walnuts were eaten year round from those trees out back. My grandparents planted a garden and canned fruits and vegetables. The memory of home canned tomato juice lingers today. Never do I find a drink that good.

We had a chicken house, so eggs were on our menu most everyday and fried chicken with gravy and fresh mashed potatoes, green beans and homemade rolls on Sunday. My granddaddy would chop those chicken heads right off with an ax, and they would run around headless, terrifying the kids. One time, I had a pet turkey, but he wasn't a friendly fellow and did frighten me. I recently watched "My Life as a Turkey" on PBS, and it brought back memories of that little bird intimidating me, until one day we had him for dinner! If you haven't seen "My Life as a Turkey," it is educational and entertaining!

Sometimes, my self sufficient grandmother made soap from saved grease and lye. It didn't smell too great, but had magical cleaning powers! I've heard that local West Virginia crafters still make and sell lye soap. I know that Doug, years ago, swore by it for cleaning his coal mining clothes! Our memories are different from those that today's children will share. Homemade butter and hams were provided by country relatives, and milk came from our cow and later a neighbor's cow. To save money, bread, pies, cakes and other desserts were homemade. Preparing apple butter was a social event with family and friends gathering for hours of cooking and stirring apples in a giant copper pot, then, ladling it into jars, after consuming quite a bit on huge chunks of bread. Yum!

We had several bee hives, so honey was a daily delight! We fried foods in lard which is pig fat! Recently, a lady from the Kaluk farms, at the farmers market offered to sell me some. I'm thinking about it. I'm not sure, but have heard that it is healthy. The taste is in my memory bank as delicious. I'm certain that I ate better and healthier when I was poor than I do now!

One day, I would work hard and provide for myself, and I did work while in college, borrowed money that I paid back and received a small amount of scholarship funds. I taught school and enjoyed it for over 30 years and began early retirement at age 55. God is good!

With Russell going away to MCA, we were temporarily off the hook for his financial needs and constant requests. But, there was a much greater need--Success! Russell's success in school and acceptance of God's help was requested in many prayers. Right away Russell got the message. The following is a letter written by me to our church that is evidence of Russell's acceptance of God's intervention in his life.

"As most of you know, Russell has behaved horribly over the past year with his decisions to move from his Mother's home, to quit school, to quit GED classes, to smoke a lot of pot, to steal from us, to be defiant to Eric who allowed him to live there until he couldn't tolerate him, to live like a slob with anyone who would let him...etc. Beth checked into various schools that he might attend and found a five month residency program in northern WV. This school is for students to work for their GED and to learn life skills. He cursed and swore that he would never go, and no one could make him. It was true that he couldn't be forced. He had to agree. Finally, after a lot of prayer, he agreed to try it for 3 weeks. On the Sunday that he left for school, Doug and I went forward in church and asked the elders to gather around us for prayer. The following Thursday, I received a letter from Russell that I am, in part, sharing:

"This school isn't near as bad as what I thought it would be. I pray every day and I remember you telling me prayer will get me through it. I'm beginning to believe you." Other letters: "this school isn't too bad. It's hard work, but hard work is what it takes to be something in life. Always remember that. Thanks for the prayers. I need them. I have actually been going to church here and everything. I pray 10-15 times a day and I think God is the only reason why I'm making it through this." Next letter..."I'm still praying everyday more than I ever have. God is amazing! I learned if you look at the positive side of things, life isn't bad. Really, I mean, I didn't want to come here, but I'm here. I told myself, Russell, you're here, so just try to stick it out. That is what I am doing, and I don't regret it one bit."

It is wonderful to have a church family to share the good and the bad. The following is a response to this letter from a church member, and I thank Carole for the powerful words: "thank you so much for your devotion today. The power of prayer!!! We all need to hear answers to prayers, especially when they affect our young ones when they are going through such horrible times. The fears of parents and grandparents, uncles…nightmares! And when Russell became a man by turning towards Our Lord…the celebration that rang out in family as well as in Heaven! Ahhhhhhh. Yep, Power of Prayers!!! Amen!!"

We praise our Lord for his many blessings! A post on Facebook says that our relationship with God should not be just a Sunday event. My hope is to move closer to Him each day. I have always told my children and grandchildren that they can have a marvelous life through Jesus Christ and prayer. Since I have moved closer to God, I am having a MARVELOUS life! God provides every need and more each moment. I have a personal relationship with Him!

A letter cut from the newspaper and attached to my refrigerator was written by John King, pastor of Johnston Chapel Baptist Church. It was published in the Bluefield Daily Telegraph for Thanksgiving 2011. It reminds us to be thankful all the time and to give thanks to God for life, health, for our material blessings, for food, shelter, clothing, our cars, and for work and for all things. He reminds us to praise God for family and friends! I am thinking of how much I love Jesus, and I am thankful always for Him! Frederick Whitfield wrote this fabulous hymn in 1855. I haven't heard it sung in a while, but my cousin Mike, recently texted that they were singing it in his church in California. The words say so much:

There is a Name I love to hear, I love to sing its' worth; It sounds like music in my ear, The sweetest Name on earth. Oh, how I love Jesus, Oh, how I love Jesus, Oh how I love jesus, Because He first loved me! It tells me of a Savior's love...

Notes 5
(Mother)

Pastor King writes that Paul reminds us in the Bible to be **"always giving thanks to God the Father for everything in the name of our Lord Jesus Christ"** (Ephesians 5:20), and to give **thanks in all circumstances, for this is God's will for you in Christ Jesus"** (1 Thessalonians 5:18). I recommend writing down the things that you are thankful for. You will be enriched by the experience. List everything, big and small. My Mother was listed first with the knowledge understood that God is actually number one. I did not have, in my mind, the typical neighborhood Mom. Yet, she taught me the most important thing of all. God is in control, and prayers are answered! We are to love Jesus Christ and one another, and only through Him can we go to heaven.

As a child, I am ashamed to say, that my Mother was an embarrassment to me many times. She adhered to Biblical scriptures that suggested that women not cut their hair and not wear makeup. She was physically ill and also blind for much of her life, and sometimes had mental health issues as well. We lived with my grandparents and times were difficult. Yet, what a huge gift from God to have a parent to bring me up in the knowledge and faith of our heavenly Savior!

She came to live our family when our daughter was two. Beth and later our son, Eric, brought a lot of joy to her life. She was very sick and handicapped. Her doctor told me when she first came to stay with us that her health was so poor he doubted she would live a year. She certainly beat those odds by living ten years in our home and two more in a nursing home. Many times we would ask her how she was feeling. Her standard answer "I'm just fine." Doug was good to provide for her when I needed a brief respite from my caregiver and teacher roles. I would escape for a mini vacation with my friend Brenda, and he would prepare meals or fulfill her fast food requests. He was a little stunned on the day that he asked what she would like to eat and her reply, "Well, a leg of lamb would be good!" Lamb with mint jelly was an occasional special treat in our home, and she didn't realize the preparation required.

I find that the words of Martin Luther King Jr. apply to my Mother. "If you can't fly, then run, if you can't run, then walk, if you can't walk, then crawl, but whatever you do, you have to keep moving forward." That was her way. One good memory is of helping her to can pickles, although I had no idea of what I was doing, and she couldn't see. Amid my protests, she directed me to complete the task that she wanted done. Many days, she crawled out of bed rather than be out of the household flow. What a glorious day it was when she went to heaven, her body so frail, but her mindset on eternal life!

On a daily basis, I see many blessings and am thankful! As I travel to meet granddaughters at their bus stop, a turkey flies across my view to a tree. Dogwood and redbud are in bloom with dandelions galore and multiple colors greet me in the hill top trees. Two precious little girl sweethearts greet me with hugs. We pass clothes drying on a clothesline, and as we reach their home a rooster crows. I bring home fresh eggs. West Virginia at its' best!

And, West Virginia at its' very best will be near the end of July. TOMATOES! The most delicious that you have ever tasted! Just buy a loaf of salt risin' or sour dough at the farmers market, cut a slice, add mayo and tomato and you have "Almost Heaven!" My son plants tomatoes each year at my request as a Mother's Day gift, and one year my son-in-law and his Mom gave me that special treat. My daughter Beth has the opposite feelings about tomatoes. As a child she complained about "tomato stains" on a sandwich that she ordered when tomato slices were mistakenly put on. Eric, though, enjoys them as much as I do. My blessings continue.

Notes 6
(Russell)

Family and friends were, in early December of 2009, tremendously pleased after rising early and traveling several hours to Kingwood WV, to celebrate Russell's GED Diploma and graduation from Mountaineer Challenge Academy. He has come a long way in 5 months. He looks fabulous marching in, and we can see the pride in his face and in our faces. When the ceremony is over, we exchange hugs and so much joy!

 We praise God for this achievement! After gathering his things, it is time for lunch at a restaurant not far from Kingwood. We have not had this many family and friends together in a long time. It is one more blessing from our Heavenly Father. Russell is looking forward to his graduation gift. His Mom and stepdad promised a car if he stuck with the program, not a new one, but a used green Jeep that he had requested. It is waiting at his parents' home in the WV Mountains. Also, Russell is turning 18 the day after graduation. There is much happiness.

 But, true to his nature, upon his return, he has no desire to live with family. After all, at age 18, he announces that he is a "man!" "Granny," he will say, "you don't need to tell me what to do anymore, I am a man now." He quickly finds various friends willing to have him stay with them. Soon, in the WV winter, he has gotten his car stuck in the snow. Who does this "man" call for help? As usual, he

Mary Feuchtenberger

would not listen to those who suggested he wait for better weather. It will be a while before he can take possession of his car, but his buddies are happy to cart him around. He has plenty of money with graduation, birthday and Christmas gifts.

Before long, he becomes the wild and wooly Russell of the past. His goal is always to live in the fastest of the fast lanes. He wants to enjoy life to the fullest, but on the wrong side of the tracks. If we try to advise him of better ways, he is quick to point out that he is a "man" now! At this point in his life, he believes that he has the freedom to do as he pleases, and it doesn't seem to matter if it hurts other people. Of course, this "man" can't really support himself. His enabling grandparents provide way too many of his needs. He works putting in pools for a friend's parents' business and earns decent pay. That seems to go well..."for a while" and he lives with these people..."for a while." He is able to use his car "for a while" with us paying the car insurance. He also works again for a fast food restaurant..."for a while." We give lots of money and he works for us. Regretfully, we do pay very well.

He begins moving further from God, and several months after graduation has a startling confrontation with the parents of a girl he has dated. Actually, they didn't date; they had a one night stand, which, unfortunately, is the norm for many young people. Russell, nervously, asks me to go with him to a nearby parking lot to meet with two people who have called and requested a meeting with him. Upon our arrival, he is confronted with an extremely irate man and woman. I have no idea what is going on and don't understand the issues. They are more than furious with Russell! They say that Russell and friends came to their home in the midnight hours and that their almost 16 year old daughter went with them without parental permission. They feel it is all his fault, and Russell is the devil in not much of a disguise.

Russell is responsible for multitudes of wrong and does seem to be on a continuous downward path almost immediately after doing so well in the National Guard school. His conduct breaks my heart again and again. These parents have huge reasons for their animosity, since their daughter and Russell had consensual sex during this time. Upon her return home, she felt traumatized by what she had done with someone she had just met and overdosed on some pills. She was hospitalized briefly and was recovering at home. Her parents said that it was her first sexual experience, and they planned to press charges, since Russell was 18 and she was 15, a few weeks shy of 16.

The father had a gun with him and told me that he was very tempted to use it on Russell. I understood the temptation, but I tried to be the calming effect and, certainly, I did agree that Russell was at fault. I told them that he was a habitual trouble maker from a Christian family who did all that they could to rehabilitate him. I explained his progress in school and pointed out that their daughter was also in the wrong. And, as I always do, I recommended prayer as a solution and mentioned how good it is to have a church family.

Two of my grandchildren get upset with me for suggesting that they pray for every problem. One recently said to me, when I asked if she was praying, "Okay Granny, I'm not in the mood to get fussed at, so just chill." Hateful words often come from their mouths in response as they say that they do pray. I ask them to work on bringing God into their lives. It is always good to ask Him for guidance and help in all that you do, and ask Him to help you make the right life choices. And ask Him to forgive you for the times you fail to obey and honor Him. Ask God to help the people around you and family and friends. Many actions of these young people are abhorrent to me and, of course, it isn't just the young. Where is their self respect and caring for others? They have been taught to obey God, but now they want only their desires.

The two greatest commandments in Matthew 22:37-40 (NIV) are as Jesus replied: **"Love the Lord your God with all your heart and with all your soul and with all your mind. This is the first and greatest commandment. And the second is like it. Love your neighbor as yourself."** You may wonder how to develop these feelings. Pray and ask God to come into your heart. Honor Him on your knees. Make it a point to give Him more time. Certainly, I intensified my walk with God after experiencing the wrath of these two parents. What person ever has to deal with the situations that I have been brought into by Russell?

Russell is again, bringing me nearer and nearer to God. Yet, I know and read of many people with much worse heartaches than ours. We did check into the legal ramifications of Russell's conduct. There was the possibility of court action, but it was unlikely. Actually, that was the last we heard of the situation. Russell was very guilty, but so was the girl. We are all sinners, yet God loves us and forgives us. It is heart breaking to see the wrong decisions of many. How do people without Christ in their life deal with it. Philippians 4:6-7 says **"Don't worry about anything; instead pray about everything. Tell God what you need, and thank him for all he has done. If you do this, you will experience God's peace, which is far more wonderful than the human mind can understand. His peace will guard your hearts and minds as you live in Christ Jesus."**

Russell constantly brings me to the Bible. Where would I be without Russell? What is the Russell in your life? Is it a son, a daughter or a cousin? Is it your own addiction, alcohol, adultery or more? There are multitudes of factors to disrupt that smooth sailing we desire. Rick Warren writes in The Purpose Driven Life that "God never does anything accidentally, and he never makes mistakes. He has a reason for everything he creates." One of the reasons that Russell is here is to bring me closer to God. So many times, I have wanted to escape this grandson whom I love, but am worn out with. Since reading the Bible and seeking this closer walk, I have been able to release much of my worry. When things do trouble me, I know that I should read scripture and pray more. This blessing can be yours if you will make that choice.

We continue to see Russell's decline. He drives his car to near destruction and finally decides to sell it. The money is needed for his developing drug habit. Maybe he has had the car for 4-5 months. We hear, and believe, but can't confirm that he drives someone's car without permission, wrecks it and people are hurt. People say that they have seen him intoxicated in public, and he appears to be very drunk or drugged.

We believe that he is similar to his Dad and want to lay blame. It is in his genes. What is the answer? Even though we know to turn to God, we agonize and forget. Often, we think, what can we do--instead of turning him over to God. We see him way too much for his money fix. He still stays with friends and doesn't visit with family. He works for us mowing the lawn and household cleaning. I appreciate the help, but I am actually buying drugs. It is really hard to pinpoint his addiction.

It took me a long time to feel certain that he had a problem. It took my husband Doug or as Russell and the other grandchildren call him, Pappy, even longer. I am the one who was around him more and felt he wasn't behaving right. His eyes would squint and actually look evil sometimes. On occasion I felt afraid of him. He would lash out inappropriately during general conversations. It was rare to see his fabulous smile.

The thought of him abusing drugs began to surface more often. A few times, I drove him to a local service station where he bought what he called legal synthetic drugs. I assumed that they were a good alternative to illegal drugs, but since that time, realize they are also bad. Our granddaughter tried them this past year and almost died, yet they are legal.

Recently, Russell told me that he began using pills after his fast food job. His marijuana use began at about age 10 when he was influenced by a young teen in his neighborhood. Now, he was in losers' splendor with loads of cash. Money was the word for him. He did love to have lots of it and to flaunt it. Drugs provided his every dream...for a while, but his life caught up with him and almost ended.

He had only been out of school for six months when his Mom called one evening. She received word from a buddy of Russell's that an ambulance had been requested and that Russell was taken unconscious to the emergency room of our local hospital. It was horrible to see him there. Drool was running from his mouth. He was nasty from vomit, feces, and urine and his survival was questionable. His Mom said that she was numb. I had cried uncontrollably since the phone call.

I do admit that at times his death seemed like a good solution to most of our problems. We were disgusted with the continual drama. We prayed for God's blessings, and Russell did recover from this near death experience to continue the life of a druggie. I asked him if he knew drug addicts who have died, and he said that he knew many. He had an aunt and an uncle and 2 cousins on his Dad's side of the family and several friends and acquaintances. He knew 10 or more people imprisoned for drug related crimes. This seems to be the norm in southern WV. It appears reasonable to me that the police would be involved in a drug overdose. However, that didn't happen. I was told that patients in hospitals have privacy rights. So he was released after spending 4-5 days in intensive care. Maybe he did better..."for a while."

We hope that he will stay off of drugs and possibly join the service. His Aunt Betse prays for him and is concerned for his well being. She emails "Russell takes such patience and a delicate, but deft approach. I second your idea of recommending the service. It would provide structure, a great income, new incentive and a goal--beyond any small odd job satisfaction he enjoys today. We'll all be so proud--just as we were when he completed the Mountaineer Challenge Academy--only a million times more! Goooo Russell!" Doug takes him several times to the recruiting station and they check online, but he really isn't interested.

Immediately, he professes to have quit using drugs and to be on the straight and narrow path. He had learned his lesson. He is a "man!" Again, he worked putting in pools for his friends and various jobs for us. He is still a good worker, but where does the money go? We get through the rest of 2010 with minimal problems, but know that Russell is still using drugs, and he cannot be trusted.

When he visits our home we literally follow him from room to room. His eyes are always looking for the prize that he can take and convert for money. We did have our annual Christmas morning breakfast with family in 2010, and Russell was included. I make it a point to prepare his favorite food which is sausage gravy along with eggs, bacon, hash browns and cinnamon rolls to insure the enjoyment of every one.

The house is decorated with a fresh cut Frasier fir tree that reaches the ceiling. We have purchased it at a tree farm not far from our home. Doug and I enjoy this annual tradition of searching for the perfect tree to cut, and we trod up and down the Spanishburg hills looking at a hundred or more before selecting the best. Trees are fabulous creations. Doug's Mom gave Eric a tree for his birthday when he was one year old. As a young boy, he enjoyed many climbs to the top of that tall pin oak. That gift was special for many years, and, as a matter of fact, we are still enjoying shade from it.

The dining room is covered with eight or nine pink feather trees that delight my fancy and decorated with loads of antique and new ornaments. Many are hand crafted by me using materials that are mostly one hundred years or more old. I love the look of vintage paper and have developed the art of making scrap ornaments. I am honored that many of my designs have been sold to others on eBay with similar interests and hopefully will grace Christmas trees for years to come. The atmosphere here is full of delight and joy. We are happy to have both of our children, their spouses and their children. We are also fortunate to have Doug's brother and sister and niece from nearby Bluefield and his younger brother Rollie and companion DJ from Washington DC. Exchange students from Germany and Belgium add to the mix, as they are part of Betse and John's family each year.

We have a great celebration of the birth of Jesus Christ!! This would be our last Christmas breakfast to include Russell..."for a while." We hope and, always pray, for his future presence. His getting together with an unknown girl is in the works. I realize that he is sneaking around, and he has concocted a story. A local grocery store parking lot is their meeting place, and he finally admits to me that she is married with a husband who is away in the service. Descriptions are fuzzy. Later, I learn the truth; that the person he was meeting is the one who later joined his demise into deceit and heartbreak.

Russell has a way of doing the wrong thing most of the time, without any caring for the consequences. The person that he is sneaking around seeing has a husband and a 2 year old son. She is the wife of someone we know. She is an exceptionally beautiful 25 year old woman. What could possibly peak her interest in Russell? She is in an unhappy marriage. Her husband and Russell have been good friends. She and Russell have been together in diverse situations and many events at his Mom's house. I think she used to cry on his shoulder when things were unhappy for her. She began to spend more and more time with Russell and talked with him about drug use. Unfortunately, drugs became a binding force between them, and to keep her happy Russell needed to be the provider. Soon their secret rendezvous was secret no more.

I saw an interesting post on social media attributed to Rock Church and also attributed to Tucker Max. It says **"the devil doesn't come dressed in a red cape and pointy horns. He comes as everything you've ever wished for. Pray for wisdom and discernment."** I don't include this to mean that she is the devil. To me, it means that evil comes from activities and material goods that we find very appealing. These wants appear beautiful to us, but in God's eyes may be wrong. To pray for discernment means just to ask God to guide you to make the right choices and to have wisdom in your decisions.

Notes 7
(Prayer)

We had barely survived 2010 with Russell returning to Princeton and reuniting with friends in situations much like the ones that caused his demise a few years before. I saw a quote recently by Joel Osteen, "you cannot expect to live a positive life if you hang with negative people." I feel sorry for the people who decided to hang with Russell, and I am sad for his choices. It is a no win relationship. The consequences begin.

Russell continues to see this beautiful woman. He professes to be in love with her, and we understand the attraction. He needs a way to support the life he hopes to have with her. Doug again urges him to join the military, but they have no place for boys like Russell, and he really doesn't want to leave our area. He decides that coal mining is a way to make a lot of money (he thinks money can buy happiness) and asks about enrolling in a class for mining papers. I agree to drive him the 40 miles to the class, and he is interviewed, and his name is on a list for possible entrance into the program. One problem is the requirement to pass a drug test, so he reluctantly decides against the class.

How will he support his woman? I still have no idea of who he is involved with. He will often tell me secrets, but not this time. Soon, after a night of partying, he is taken to the emergency room of the local hospital with a broken jaw. I am very alarmed and upset. He says that someone sucker punched him, and he doesn't even know who did it, because he was so messed up from alcohol and drugs. He has no health insurance and no doctor to repair it.

Since Beth works at this hospital, she inquires on what can be done. The advice is to go to West Virginia University (WVU) in Morgantown. They are a teaching school and hospital, and he can have his jaw wired free of charge. Doctors insist that this needs to be done immediately to avoid lifelong problems. They advise that the other side can break due to the wrong pressure being applied with one side already broken.

Phone calls are made and much paperwork is completed to facilitate this as quickly as possible. Beth makes arrangements to be off work and finds baby sitters for her 2 little girls. I agree to go with her. Russell says that he really doesn't want to go, but we convince him of the need. Our first appointment is on Thursday February 24, 2011 for a consultation with doctors who can wire the jaw.

We tell him that we will pick him up early to make our appointment, but at our agreed time and place, he is not to be found. Why does this not surprise me? Why do we care? WVU, in Morgantown, is a 4 hour drive, and we are becoming stressed after calling and searching for him for over an hour. He is finally located, and we drive to the hospital. The doctors examine, x-ray, and schedule surgery for the following Tuesday. He is told to only eat liquids to prevent problems, but he insists on solid food when we stop to eat. It is beyond his ability to listen to those in authority or anyone trying to tell him what to do. After all, he is a "man" now!

Also, it is hard to believe, but he described to the doctors his excruciating jaw pain, and they provided strong pain medicine for him to take home. I never ever saw him in pain or complain other than to the doctor. As soon as we got home, he brazenly said that he is going to sell the pain medicine, and we drop him off at his requested location. After that long, miserable day with him, we were happy to have him out of our space. We had come home in the kind of pouring down rain that makes dangerous driving and traumatizes. We only wanted the comforts of home. Beth was drained physically and mentally, but had to be up the next morning before 6 to get the kids ready for school and to go to work. Russell never has a kind word for her. Many times he shouts at her and uses mean and hateful language. Her hurt is often evident in conversations about him.

Despite all her efforts to help him, he shows no respect! Part of his attitude is drugs and part is his personality. He is such an ungrateful child, but love for him is constant, regardless of his ugliness to her. He should be thankful, as in the words of Abraham Lincoln, "I remember my mother's prayers and they have always followed me. They have clung to me all my life." Think about it, Russell.

While at the hospital, we realize that our problems are small compared to those of others. We saw many sick children and one in particular with horrible physical deformities and, probably, mental inabilities being maneuvered in a wheelchair. Through tears, I prayed for them and praised the Almighty Lord for our many blessings! When we see others with needs, it is good to ask God to provide for them.

We are told in Thessalonians 5:17, to **pray without ceasing**. You may wonder how to do this? Once you move close to God you will know. Don't wait until before you go to bed to say your prayers. When you see or think of a need just talk to Him, and thank Him for everything during the day. It is a part of me. Thank you Lord for that parking place! Oh Lord, help that lady over there. Please bless that person on social media who requested prayer. Thank you for my children and grandchildren. Help me to make the best decision on a new car. Guide that person to give up drugs. Bless the little ones in church and their families. Throughout the day I chat with God.

On a recent visit with my uncle, he complained of horrible tooth pain and said that he had called and couldn't find a dentist to give him an appointment. Now, this is my 97 year old uncle, and I could barely tolerate the thought of his agony. He called several dentist offices, and I tried to find one who would see him, but all of them were booked for several weeks. I left his home in tears. As I was driving, I became angry with myself. Why? I had failed to pray. I had tried to control the situation myself and was getting angry with the doctors. I stopped the car and called his pastor immediately and requested prayer and knew that God would provide. My uncle had an appointment made the next day! Rejoice!!! God is good all of the time. All of the time God is good! Prayer should be continuous, and it is very easy and rewarding to develop this habit.

True to his nature, Russell has not completed the paperwork for his jaw surgery. They have called here two times and say they can only talk with him....since he is a man now! He refuses to return their calls until the very last minute. He only cares about drugs and his woman. His broken jaw has no meaning. A few days pass, and it is time to return to Morgantown to have his jaw wired. I am just going to include a copy of the email that I sent to my cousin regarding this event.

Notes 8
(Letter)

I guess that it is time to write. I feel that we are on a death watch here. On Tuesday, Beth and Timmy took Russell to Morgantown (4 hour drive), and I kept their girls. Doctors wired his jaws together and wanted him to stay the night. He absolutely refused! They returned by 10:00 pm because Russell had a woman he wanted to see. By morning, he has had another altercation. His jaw appears to be broken again! This relationship with the beautiful woman is not good. They are continuing to see each other and seem to be doing a lot of drugs. We do not know where the drug money comes from. We are afraid of him because we know that drugs and women have caused young men to do horrible crimes. Possibly someone would like to kill Russell for his actions! It is so hard to believe the evil that comes from drug abuse. Russell just told me on Thursday that he needed in residence drug treatment, but he is too flighty to pin down. Just getting the jaw fixed for "free" cost $600.00 with 2 trips and prescriptions, and Beth and Timmy missed

Mary Feuchtenberger

work. Luckily, I had just made $700 on eBay and was able to pay, but I hate to waste time and money. We think that rehab would be the same thing, but we are checking. This is so hard to deal with, and we do need divine intervention. Please pray for us.

Notes 9
(Blessings)

That black cloud over our head is getting bigger and bigger, darker and darker. Beth and all of our family want to help Russell with a drug rehab program. Various treatment centers are checked into. The local hospital has a place you can sign in for help and Russell agrees. Yes, he says, he will be right there and needs help. Yet, he is never available when it is time to be admitted.

Beth writes to an advertised email address with a television show called Intervention. Probably, many of you have watched it, and some people appear to be helped with this program. When we watch, we see that so many other families have druggies in their lives and much of the trauma is the same. Lying, stealing, overdosing, shouting, cursing, money demands and denial are common denominators. We are surprised to receive notification from the producers that they may accept us for an intervention. Oh WOW, we are going to be on TV, but mainly we are so hopeful of help. They send us explicit instructions.

Under no circumstances is Russell to know it is a planned intervention. We are told to say that a documentary is being made about drug use, and the show would like Russell to share his experiences. Also, two family members are asked to video their answers to a set of questions that they have emailed. We make a videotape with Russell detailing his drug use. Then, Beth and

I discuss the questions and send the videos to their address. This is called the Courage to Share project, and we all believe that we have done a great job. Beth gets a phone call that the producers plan to use our story for the television show, and soon I get a phone call from a Los Angeles number confirming details. Everything is in place, and we are very excited for an intervention. Then, we wait and wait and hope and hope and never hear from them again! This is such a huge disappointment. We assume that there are many requests, and one that was more appealing was used.

We have an excellent local Christian drug treatment program called Teen Challenge, and Beth inquires about it. They send the paperwork and we complete it with much information, but it never gets used for various reasons. Russell has to be in agreement to go, and he hasn't reached that point.

Beth's husband Timmy has always wanted to help Russell. Early in his relationship with Beth he tried to help control his defiant and aggressive behavior, and Russell responded well ... for a while. We now know that most of the problem was drugs and that they take over some people completely, as was the case with Russell. God is the answer. There is a lot of stress involved when anyone is using drugs. We are a family who all love and care for Russell and try every way possible to help him.

We continue to keep Russell on the prayer list at church. Most people are on this list for 3 weeks, but he has been on the list for several years. We do not think he would be with us if not for prayer. We draw closer to God because of our problems. The Bible (Psalm 34:18, NLT) states **"The Lord is close to the broken hearted; he rescues those who are crushed in spirit."** So many positives have come from prayer, but with the present drug use it is hard to see. He did graduate Mountaineer Challenge Academy. He did acknowledge that God helped him. He did survive a near drug overdose. Thank you God! We again turn to our church for help. We schedule a meeting with our pastor for advice. It is good to voice our concerns, and prayer is still the answer.

Groundhog Day in West Virginia

If we go to our Bible, we can find peace in our hearts. Again, I use this verse. Philippians 4:6-7 (NKJV) provides comfort. **"Be anxious for nothing, but in everything by prayer and supplication with thanksgiving let your requests be made known to God and the peace which surpasses all comprehension will guard your hearts and your minds in Christ Jesus."** Russell is bringing me to the Bible one more time.

The ups and downs I have with letting go of the worry of Russell is sad. It means I need more faith when I worry. As James 4:8 says **"draw close to God and he will draw close to you**." And also Luke 1:37 reminds us that Faith does not make things easy. It makes them possible. I get away from Him and the worry begins. Shame on me! It is always a joy to draw close, and it fosters an enriched life. For me and for many, it is good to have a routine of time to connect with God. The more you do that, the more you will want to. Begin your day praising Him and reading the Bible. God wants us to have fellowship with other Christians. Find a church, and within that church will be many opportunities to learn of Jesus Christ and share your blessings and concerns.

Bible study is great! You can meet in small groups and have the word of God explained. Many churches offer Bible lessons. Just call and check or look on their website. I have generally had a hard time understanding much of the Bible. Study groups have been extremely helpful. When I was a child I would read the Bible to my Mother each day. She was blind, but faithful to The Lord with my help.

I love the quote attributed to Martin Luther: `"The Bible is alive; it speaks to me. It has feet; it runs after me. It has hands; it lays hold of me!"`

My prayer is that the Bible will speak to you and to me and lay hold of us! Today there are several versions of the Bible, and some may suit you better than the standard King James Version. I like the New King James Version, the Contemporary English Version, the New International Version, the New Living Translation and The Message. Other versions are also good. My phone has several Bible apps, and the one that I use gives me numerous versions of each Bible verse. It is a free app that I enjoy and use frequently. It shows a Bible labeled Holy Bible.

Many television pastors give excellent Bible explanations and their videos and books can be purchased, and some are free. I enjoy Bobby Schuller, David Jeremiah, Kerry Shook, Max Lucado and others. It took me awhile to listen to Joyce Myers because at first glimpse she didn't appeal to me. She is a very feisty lady! Now, I love to hear her messages and have purchased several of her books. Powerful stuff!!

How many times do you scroll through your TV stations and say that nothing is on. Make your television a tool for God's word! Move close to Him! You will be amazed at the testimonies of many. Recently, I saw Jake Olson on Hour of Prayer with Bobby Schuller. At the time he was a teenager in high school who had, not long before, lost all of his eyesight. His accomplishments and positive attitude are astonishing. He has written a book titled Open Your Eyes that will help......open your eyes.

Be a family with your family. Plan events together and include going to church. God wants you! In Matthew 18:20 (KJV) is a fabulous reason for being in a church. **"For where two or three are gathered together in my name, there am I in the midst of them."** Gives me chills! He is with you in the midst with your fellow Christian friends.

Social media has reunited me with many Christian friends, and we ask each other for prayer. Shenia, a former student, and I remain close because we both love Our Heavenly Father. We count on each other as prayer warriors. Garnetta, a long time friend, is always good to offer encouraging messages. Charletta posted one of the kindest commendations recently! Barbie, Randall and Chad from my church family provide inspiration often with their messages. In a recent post, a mother was in the hospital with her dying child. She petitioned God, as did others for her child. Angels appeared and white images were seen by many surrounding her daughter who had a miraculous recovery. There are angels among us.

Look around and count your blessings and see what God has done. Do you know that hymn? Singing is a wonderful part of worshiping God. There are many hymns that bring joy to me and some bring tears. Count Your Blessings was published in 1897 by Johnson Oatman Jr. The words printed here are worthy of deep consideration.

When upon life's billows you are tempest tossed, when you are discouraged, thinking all is lost, count your many blessings, name them one by one, and it will surprise you what The Lord hath done. Count your blessings, name them one by one. Count your blessings. See what God hath done! Count your blessings, name them one by one. Count your many blessings. See what God hath done.

And it will surprise you what The Lord hath done. Are you ever burdened with a load of care? Does the cross seem heavy you are called to bear? Count your many blessings, every doubt will fly, and you will keep singing as the days go by.

I cannot sing a lick as the old saying goes. I'm sure, though, that my children and grandchildren will remember my efforts to sing to them. One of my favorites was My Gal's A Corker. I also sang Shortnin Bread and Little Cabin in the Woods. And, I still enjoy "Hush Little Baby…Mockingbird" and sang it for my kids and grandkids. I do have odd tastes in my choices, but they are fun songs. And, I always included a few hymns like Jesus Loves Me. When I hear myself sing in church I am embarrassed. God doesn't care. So, I do as best I can, and occasionally belt one out when I am alone at home. I enjoy listening to gifted singers and love hearing old hymns. It is about worshiping God and our efforts to please Him.

Notes 10
(Travel)

The summer of 2011 was not easy. Much of it was spent trying to accommodate Russell, and some time was used attempting to escape from his needs. Often, he would come to our home with a friend, and I would cook for them. He would bring his dirty clothes for me to wash and would bathe and change clothes here. Sometimes, he and his friend needed a ride, and I was their taxi. They helped me by working on household needs, but money was their goal. More and more, I saw evil in Russell's face. More and more I became fearful. Finally, I decided that he could not visit if Doug was not at home. There are far too many newscasts with stories of drug induced crimes. We purchased pepper spray and a shock device to give me some security.

Unknown to me, but to relieve me of Russell's daily harassment, Doug began paying Russell's stepmom to allow him to live with her. She has 4 young children and a live in boyfriend. It seems a difficult environment for everyone in a small mobile home. Her Pit Bull bites Russell after a confrontation between him and her boyfriend, and he requires treatment at the hospital emergency room. Following that event, he needs a new place to live and finds a friend or two that he can pay or we can pay to keep him away.

We are facing changes in our life. Doug is looking forward to his last day of work. Actually, I am looking forward to it more than he is. His official retirement begins October 1, 2011, and he is showered with love and respect at his retirement party. Everyone made sure that he knew how valuable he was to them and that he will be missed. I joke that "I'm working on the "honey do and the bucket lists!" I have planned for us a driving trip to California. Doug is ready to go! Giving up his job has been very traumatic and he wants to "get out of Dodge."

Just days before our planned departure, our druggie grandson breaks our hearts. He calls to ask his Pappy to bring him some food from a local fast food place. And, we cater his needs. While Doug is gone to get the food, he cuts the lock on our storage area and steals our lawn mower. We do not yet know of the theft, as he stops by for the food and merrily leaves with a friend. He is so uncaring, and drugs have made him a horrible person. Soon, we realize what has happened and, of course, he pleads innocence. But we know that he has taken it. This causes very much sadness. It is time to get an order of protection.

We are still worried that he will break into our home while we are traveling, but we have very watchful neighbors, and Beth and Eric agree to check on our home every day. Oops, did I say we were worried? Psalm 91:14-16 (The Message) has words to strongly take to heart and consider. **"If you'll hold on to me for dear life, says God, "I'll give you the best of care if you'll only get to know and trust me. Call me and I'll answer, be at your side in bad times; I'll rescue you, then, throw you a party. I'll give you a long life, give you a long drink of salvation!"** The rewards are many for those who are faithful to God!

Our trip of a lifetime begins on October 7, 2011. We are in no hurry and go only as far as Corydon IN the first day. It is a little more than halfway to St Louis. When Doug was working, we traveled to Corydon for dinner and a day of antiquing several times. It was 365 miles, and we would stay one night and drive back home. We both liked the drive and the time together.

I am looking forward to visiting family in St. Louis, and the next day we enjoy seeing cousins and having a scrumptious dinner with

Mary Feuchtenberger

my favorite food…mashed potatoes! I think that we also had steak, but that part didn't matter. I love my St. Louis family! When Eric had his learners' license, I let him drive me to St. Louis. He wanted to see a Cardinals' baseball game, and it was a great bonding experience, plus we reunited with cousins! Only, recently, as a grown man, did he tell me how frightening the drive was for him. I believed that he was an excellent driver traveling through construction, multiple lanes of city traffic and hard to reach exits. And, I was happy to be driven…clueless!

Doug and I drive through Kansas on our way to Glenwood Springs in Colorado. Here, we enjoy swimming in a two block long hot tub and pool. The sun is out with a little melting snow. The Rocky Mountains are spectacular, but somewhat scary with huge rocks high above the road. Thank you God for protecting us!

The Great Salt Lake in Utah is splendid and their red rock parks are to die for! Previously, we traveled to Bryce, Zion and the Arches parks in Utah and their beauty brought tears to my eyes. I generally chat with the young Latter Day Saints missionaries from Utah when they visit our town and always communicate my joy of traveling in their state. Likewise, they complimented our Mountain State, West Virginia.

We go out of our way to visit Crater Lake in Oregon. Thank you God for nudging us! Perfect blue water and astonishing landscape met our every gaze. Later, we make it to Crescent City in CA. After checking our motel room and going out for grocery needs, we drive by a little beach road that we decide to venture onto. Thank you God again and again!!! We weren't expecting this, but He dropped it in our laps. The beach sunset of all sunsets!!! It was outstanding in beauty! We knew that we were blessed!

The next day, we drove through the redwoods and through a redwood. Yes, a huge redwood has been carved so that a car can drive through it. The trees are overwhelming and were a main reason for making our trip to California. My friend, Hal, had described to me their beauty and special emotional appeal. Yet, we didn't go to Muir Woods that he had recommended…maybe next time. The redwoods are spectacular and worth repeat trips to fully enjoy their enormity and beauty.

God's majesty is revealed again and again. We weren't crazy about the traffic on the Golden Gate Bridge in San Francisco, but we survived it and were blessed to travel the highway of Big Sur. A childhood, Wallace Street friend, Bobby, who lives in California suggested we visit there. And, though it was difficult to locate, we arrive at paradise in the form of Pfeiffer Beach. It is hard to believe the differences in Pfeiffer Beach and the Carolina beaches that we are used to, with warm water and flat landscape. Massive rock formations are numerous at Pfeiffer and the water is cold, but it is a splendid beach. I said, that now, I understand why people stay in California, even if it does have earthquakes. The beauty takes my breath away! Thank you God! We are counting our blessings...one by one and they continue.

We begin our journey back east and make sure to return to Sedona, AZ. We had visited there three years before, when we celebrated my 60th birthday, with my desire to see the Grand Canyon. Sedona is near there and has gorgeous red rock and good restaurants and is an easy drive. An interesting part of the Sedona trip was connecting with people who were staying in the same motel. We had decided to use the pool and found only one other couple in the water. They were probably twenty five years younger, and I was intimidated by how the woman looked in a bathing suit. Surely we had nothing in common, and I was swimming at the opposite end of the pool. Doug, who is usually Mr. Antisocial, instigated a conversation with the man, and they had some shared interests. However, the amazing bond was their faith in God. It is wonderful to have fellowship planned and provided by God.

Sadly, we had another thing in common. They had traveled from Ohio to bring their son to drug rehab. We spoke of dealing with similar drug related experiences and our faith. For many months I prayed for their son, and I feel sure that they prayed for Russell. It was a blessing to have fellowship, and a reminder to share, even to extend a hand in friendship to that unknown person.

Mary Feuchtenberger

Our next stop, highly recommended by my cousin Mike, was Monument Valley. I can't say enough about the rock formations and aura. Old cowboy movies do no justice to this amazing Native American territory. If you haven't seen it, goggle it soon. Explore America even if only on television and in books! God's creations are mind blowing and, of course, other countries are worth a trip or two. I'm planning on seeing them when I get to heaven.

After a few more days of travel we return home. We had driven 6447 miles and never had one day of bad weather. We had missed heavy snow in Colorado and a tornado in Kansas and downpours in Tennessee. Do you wonder why? We don't. Praises! Praises! Praises to our Almighty God! We had a blessed trip, but it is good to be back at home. It was kept safe, but Eric's was not. The lock on his storage building was cut while they were at work and his new lawn mower was taken. We know the thief. The drug habit must be fed.

On Sunday November 7, 2011 we attend church with Beth and her daughters. Beth whispers to me that she wants to go forward in church and ask for prayer. She asks for the elders to gather and pray for Russell. God responds quickly. On November 13, he is put in jail for stealing. It is a way to end his evil and we are thankful. On November 15, Beth calls to say that she has spoken with Russell by phone, and he is praising God. He says that he needs to be in jail, and that he has gone to church there, and is praying and feeling good. Thank you Lord!

Notes 11
(Letters)

It is a week away from Christmas 2011. Our grandson will not be with us for this year's celebration of Christ's birth. This is the first year without him. Our family is glad and, also, sad for his absence. We have peace from the drama and relief from the hurt that drug use causes. We have sorrow for his chosen life and look forward to a better future. He is 20 years old and has been in jail for one month. Thank you God! We still choose not to communicate with Russell. It is good to have separation from him and his needs. I finally decide to write him a letter, the text of which follows here:

```
Dear Russell,

   I know that you are where you need to be, but
your life still breaks my heart. Much of what
you did was the drugs and not you. However, it
is hard to think that I will ever trust you.
You must try to get close to The Lord. Give
Him a lot of your time. Just talk with Him and
thank Him for everything he has given you. The
devil put you in jail, not Our Lord. You can
still have a wonderful life, but only through
Christian living. Never deny The Lord. Always
```

be proud that you believe in Him. He knows your heart and you will need to work on that. Continually ask The Lord to help you give up the evil in your life. I ask him every day to help me and you and each of us. Think of other people and their needs. Be thankful that you can see and have good health and a family who loves you. Look at the good and not the bad.

One of the main writers of the Bible, Paul, spent many horrible years in jail, but wrote of the goodness of God and to always keep faith. Even for people who are in jail for their whole life, it is just a speck. They can have a wonderful life in heaven if they will accept Christ. You need to remember that!

You wanted to do many wrong things and have fun, fun, fun. Money is NOT the way to happiness. Christ is! The devil will always try to win you back. It is a daily thing to resist evil. Everyone has to work at it.

Pray for each person who you know needs help. Ask The Lord to come into their life and show them the way. Pray for your stepmom Anna and her children, your brothers and sister. Don't rush through your prayers. Many people do, myself included. Establish a personal relationship with God where you talk with him throughout the day and thank him. Give Christ time. He wants you! Try to exercise and stay healthy. Don't just lie around. Read and do what you can to improve. We will always love you. You will have to wait to hear from Pappy. XXOO Granny

Doug and I both struggle with the decision of reconnecting with Russell. He does call, but we have to accept the call and agree to pay for it. We hear a message that says "an inmate from Southern Regional Jail is calling, and do we agree to have the call billed to our credit card?" We refuse for several months. He has written and asked for forgiveness.

After a week in jail he writes to our son Eric and daughter-in-law Shawna. He says that he is sorry for all the pain he caused and the hurt he put them through. He admits to using three to five pills a day at a cost of $75 per pill. He says that he doesn't know or understand why he did the drugs, but knows that they caused him to only think of himself and where the next pill was coming from. While it will take time, he hopes for forgiveness and another chance of their communicating with him and having a good relationship.

In his letter to me he apologizes and tells me that he is praying and trying to get closer with The Lord. He says that he will absolutely never again use drugs! He is feeling better than he has since his pill use escalated and realizes how much hurt he has caused. He asks for a Bible and says that he is reading a book about strengthening Christian faith. He again says he doesn't understand how he turned out the way he did, and that he wasn't raised that way. I sent Russell a copy of `A Purpose Driven Life`, and he professes to be reading and enjoying it.

Russell is hurt to realize that his sisters may think he is an awful person, since he is in jail. He has heartache from missing them so much. Kylie is almost 6 and has an unconditional love for her brother. Despite the fact that he is 13 years older, they have a real bond and much love for one another. Kendra, who is 4, loves him, but their connection isn't as strong. He writes many letters and constantly begs for forgiveness and states how very sorry he is for all the hurt. He will never ever do drugs again. He constantly pleads for forgiveness and professes to honor Christ and total commitment to clean living.

Countless letters continue, and I finally do answer that phone call. It is good to hear my grandson and to again feel the caring and love return. His Pappy isn't quite ready, but soon does agree to talk with him. They work out some differences and through prayer and time, we are able to reconnect. Thank you God!

Notes 12
(Family)

Of course, everything comes from God. Some things we take for granted and may forget at times to be thankful for, but others just blow me away. One is rather humorous. I am hosting a dinner party to celebrate Doug's parents' 60th wedding anniversary. We are having it in our home, and I thought it would add a great touch if I could play some of their favorite music on our jukebox. The jukebox itself is a blessing. For some reason, I got it in my head that I would love to have a jukebox. I checked on eBay and the cost was prohibitive, and I could not find one locally. Later, in looking through the trading journal for our area, there it was at a price I could afford. And, it turned out to be a friend of Doug's who gave us a good deal, and we are still enjoying it.

I asked my sister-in-law for suggestions on what to play for the dinner party. She said that "Little Brown Jug" by Glenn Miller was one of her parents' favorite songs. It is a fat chance that this child of the 60's would have a Glenn Miller record, so I checked at an antique shop with records, but no luck. Then I checked eBay and no luck. Drat! I remembered some 45's in the attic that I had purchased at a yard sale the previous year, so I looked through them. Surprisingly, there were some Glen Millers, but no "Little Brown Jug". I looked at each record, front and back. Now it is hard to believe, because I am meticulous, and there is no way that I have that record. However, I did decide to check one last time. There it is!! Thank you God! You cannot imagine the smile and joy on their faces and mine as that song was playing when they walked through our door.

Little things, big things, in all things, God is good all of the time! We had a fabulous celebration of a Christian marriage and a great coming together of children and grandchildren on that winter day in January 2002. Russell is only 10 years old and loves his great grandparents. He flashes that beautiful smile and melts their hearts as he congratulates them on their many years of marriage.

Family is extremely important! After the loss of Doug's father and later his Mom, it was time to divide some family heirlooms among their 4 children. This was done very well without dispute. However, I was disappointed. I had coveted their oriental rug. Coveting is a sin, and I was very guilty of it. I believed that the rug would make our dining room beautiful beyond compare. It had the perfect colors that I had dreamed of for the room. The problem was that Doug's younger brother, Rollie, also wanted the rug, and it was best that he have it. It was beautiful in his Washington DC home which has rare antique crown molding and perfect decor. I finally came to terms with the fact that the rug would not grace our floor, and I purchased a good looking one from a discount store. But, I did soon tire of it and decided to invest in a better quality oriental rug.

In discussing this with my brother-in-law John, he commented that he wasn't sure that Rollie was totally happy with his Mother's rug. The color wasn't right for the room. Maybe, I should ask if he was interested in selling it. We had previously found that exchanging money added to the fairness of dividing family treasures. Voila! Yes, yes, yes! He was happy to part with the rug, since he was still paying on one that he previously used and found better suited to the room. Thank you God!

And guess what? This rug did not make our dining room the most beautiful or fabulous, as I had thought it would. It looks appropriate, and we are glad for it, but it does not stand out as spectacular as I had envisioned. It is attractive and special inside our hearts, for it was a wedding gift to Doug's parents from his grandmother. We love our family, and we enjoy having heirlooms. The best holidays are ones celebrated with family, and nothing is better than our vacations together, preferably at Myrtle Beach. Traditions are built and savored with family, and we yearn for Russell's return.

Being in church with family is important and was not a consistent factor in Russell's life. It is important for people to learn of God at a young age. Proverbs 22:6 says to train up a child in the way of The Lord and when they are old they will not stray from it. Russell does know God, and he continues to be the reason for much of my connection to God.

We continue in prayer for Russell, and we are very aware that you need to watch what you pray for. I will always remember going to a church circle meeting with my grandmother when I was about 10 years old. These women obviously loved being together and were talking about prayer and the need to be careful when you pray. One lady said that during World War II, she would pray that her son would not be required to enter the armed services for fear that he would be hurt or killed. Her prayers were answered when her son was in a tractor accident, and his leg had to be amputated. She berated herself for her prayers and cautioned each person. Watch what you pray for! I pray that the Lord will bless Russell and guide him to lead a Christian life! And, I pray that for every person!

Notes 13
(Jail)

We begin reestablishing a relationship with Russell by phone calls and occasional letters. He requests money so that he can buy food and toilet items at the prison commissary. We send a small amount. Sometimes we mail books that he has requested. He seems fairly content being there. The prison has tremendous overcrowding that can't be helped. My heart aches for so many who are imprisoned, and I pray that God will guide them.

Drugs have led to much crime in southern WV. Russell knows many of the people incarcerated, and they develop a routine of activities that includes watching TV, playing cards, using the phone and eating. He isn't keen on the food, and often purchases Ramen noodles and enjoys them. Disputes break out, and he says it is important to appear strong and dominant. Basically he has adapted to the situation with only a few days of unhappiness. His court case is on slow speed, and he seldom has contact with his lawyer.

We do wonder when he will go to court, since he has been in jail for so long. We could pay his bail for just a small fee, but do not trust the consequences of his freedom. He has been in jail for 7 months without anything done about seeking a trial for his crime of stealing. The court system is tremendously over worked. We are sick with dread when he calls his Mom in early June of 2012. We all have had a very tiring day. I arrived at her house at 5:30 that morning to keep her two girls. She was ready for work and soon departed to be there at 6:00. Her husband had left even earlier that morning at 5:00 for his work at a wood products company. By evening we were all very much exhausted.

Surprisingly, Russell calls and excitedly announces "Come and get me!" And he wants us right now, right now, and I understand his elation. He says that they have dropped all charges. How can that be possible, and what are we supposed to do at 8:30 in the evening? I am worn out and about ready for bed. Honestly, it is very hard to believe and to understand that they release him that late in the evening and unexpectedly. Beth and I are traumatized. Timmy stays home with their girls, and I reluctantly agree to go with her to pick up Russell. Southern Regional Jail is 40+ miles from my house and 50+ from hers. It is dark and the WV Turnpike has much construction and traffic and heavy rain begins. It is a slow, difficult drive, and we miss our exit. We are highly stressed and wonder--what on earth are we going to do once we get him?

Neither of us feels comfortable allowing him to stay in our homes. We still do not trust him after his 7 months away, so I decide that I will pay for him to stay in a motel for a few days until a better decision can be made. We inform Doug and decide to call and tell Eric. Just a few weeks before going to jail, Russell had cut Eric's lock and taken his lawn mower and weed eater, and we want him to be aware of Russell's release.

As we are nearing the prison to get Russell we receive a phone call. It is him directing us to a gas station just a short way from the jail. This again stuns me. He has been released with a few items and authorities say goodbye, you are on your own. I can say for certain that I do not want to live near that jail if that is what they do with newly released inmates. He had no visible sign of anyone providing help or picking him up when he was let go. How is a person like that to be trusted? I guess it is the law that an "innocent" person can't be held, and since charges were dropped he was released. He is obviously ecstatic when we reach the gas station, and we are obviously not ecstatic.

Groundhog Day in West Virginia

I believe cigarettes are his first request and then a pizza. We suffer thunderstorms, limited visibility, construction and darkness once again as we drive home. He is on a natural high and borrows my phone to reconnect with his friends as we travel. While on the way, he decides to call Eric. Obviously they have a good conversation. Eric and Shawna agree that he can stay with them. They are offering him another chance. They are saints! Our worry level plummets, and we drop him off at Eric's house and return to our homes exhausted with concern for the future.

Of course we enable him to have a phone and a few other personal items. He needs a job, so he completes an employment form with an agency and is soon hired. He is given work at the same place as his stepdad with different hours and more manual labor. We are proud of him! It is just his cup of tea! He is a hard worker and is glad to work overtime. Many compliments are conveyed to his family about his work ethic. We are fortunate that Eric has a neighbor employed at the same place and willing to drive him the 5-6 miles to work. Everything is going amazingly well. After only several weeks, he receives a small pay raise.

However, come payday that money quickly disappears, and he admits to buying expensive shoes and clothes. Soon his ride to work moves out of town and that is a problem, since he works until midnight. Another ride is found, but he comes out of his way to get Russell, and we pay him. Somehow, Russell never has the funds for that, although he is well paid. At times this ride is not available, and Doug and I each take him and pick him up. Enough of that, I protest, I am no longer a taxi! Finally, Doug purchases a scooter that is allowed on the highway without a license due to its slow driving speed. We definitely are not willing to provide funding for a car plus insurance. The scooter may be a good solution, but it is an investment of one-thousand dollars.

From time to time I begin to see that little squint in his eyes. And, I hear him on the phone shouting at people. Work problems are beginning. Eric and he have differences, and he doesn't want Russell living there. He stays with friends and is always requesting money. This Bible verse is so appropriate. Proverbs 26:**11 As a dog returns to his own vomit, so a fool repeats his folly**. When I told Doug that this was an appropriate quote for Russell, he said "No, it is not. It is appropriate for a drug user." Russell is a druggie again. I remember all those letters from prison. He would never, ever, ever use drugs again, and he was reading the Bible and praying. **Move close to God and he will move close to you.** James 4:8. Who moved?

Almost immediately, God was out of Russell's life after his release from prison. Do you only move close when you need help? I admit that I do try to move closer when I have a need. I pray more and my Bible becomes a greater priority. Again and again, Russell brings me closer and closer. Even though I know the value of prayer and reading my Bible, I can always do better. I want everyone to know how wonderful a life they can have through Jesus Christ.

Amazing enjoyment each day can come from the simplest things. Point in case...Doug and I both enjoy a fire in our fireplace. When we were looking at a home to purchase over 40 years ago, we agreed that it must have a fireplace. Recently on a cold wintry day, Doug built a fire and I jokingly said "now all we need is snow" because that is truly what I love...a fire in the fireplace and snow falling outside. This is hard to believe, but is the truth. The sun was shining brightly and there had been just the tiniest bit of flurries earlier, but Doug said he would just say a prayer, and ask God to give me the snow that I wanted. Wham!!! It was immediate! Thank you God!! Pouring down beautiful snow and a fire!!

God is good all of the time. All of the time, God is good. That reminds me of another small, but delightful gift from God. It is one of those things that I coveted for awhile. Victorian calling cards are beautiful and come in hundreds of styles. They are small cards from the late 1800's with designs and names written on them like today's business cards. Many are embossed and have fancy cut trim all around. They only cost a dollar or two, sometimes a little more. I purchased one that I fell in love with. It had an embossed flower design and very special cut trim, and I coveted more.

Groundhog Day in West Virginia

  I searched eBay every day for this perfect card. I saw countless numbers of cards, but never even one card like my favorite. I looked and looked at more and more. I was obsessed with it to no avail, so I hunted an embossing tool with this design. I thought I would make my own if I had this tool, but no such instrument exists. Several months went by with continual searching...and coveting. Finally, I let it go. Many months later, that card came to mind. I was on eBay and typed it in. There it was---Fifty unused cards, my favorites! I have never ever seen ANY unused Victorian calling cards of any design much less 50 of the very ones I wanted. I bid, and they were mine.

  What have I done with them? I look at them and I smile, and I have decorated one or two. They are pretty, and I like them. My Father in heaven gave them to me. He knew that they would make me happy. As I think of this gift, tears come to my eyes. God is so good to me. I am writing this from the beach. We are on our family vacation without Russell. We are having a marvelous time!! Doug worked hard to pay for this trip. It was planned, and it did come from our Lord. Doug actually enjoys his job and likes to share with the kids and with God. The money came from Him, and we give it back. Think about tithing.

Notes 14
(Decline)

Yes, Russell has again succumbed to drug addiction! Part of his excuse to me is that no one wanted to be his friend after his release from jail. Of course, he isn't interested in people with decent life styles and Christian values. He returned to the woman he believes he loves and to his previous relationships with drug abusing friends. It brings him much happiness…for a while. While I criticize, I do know that addiction is a disease. It takes a mighty force to overcome and I feel that the only cure is a close relationship with God.

Russell's work abilities are declining as his drug use is escalating. He tries to hold it all together, but the signs are catching up with him. I, again, can barely tolerate it. Russell brings me to my knees pleading for his salvation. I want his soul for The Lord. His downfall causes tremendous heartache. The journal entry from August of 2012 attests to my broken spirit. I write that he has consumed all of my time and energy for days. He needs food, money, a ride, clean clothing, water, and screams about his difficulties. We continue paying him to mow and trim our yard. He gets it done quickly and then asks for a ride to a friend's house on Low Gap. No one needs friends like that! We have finally realized that this is his drug source. No longer will we take him there, but he finds a way.

It is very difficult for me to feel joy with his downward spiral. His actions are a repeat of his past. His visit the next day reveals a huge knot on his forehead. Again, my heart aches and sadness comes with uncontrollable sobbing and pouring down tears. Yet, as much as I love this child, I am afraid of him. He brings his girlfriend one evening, and they sit outside on our porch steps. They are talking for a long time and, I think, planning how he will do it. I know that he is always searching for money to purchase drugs, and I have a bad gut feeling about this visit. Recently, I felt that he was ready to grab my purse, but he saw me closely watching his eyes. I let him know that I mistrusted him by hugging my purse tightly to my chest. I wonder if he intends to harm me this time to get what he needs.

 I feel certain that this is the day he will try to break that barrier. Drug addicts only care about their next fix. I believe that if I open my front door to see why he is here, he will force his way in. We no longer allow him inside our home, but do pass things to him. Doug is not at home, so I am susceptible. I decide to go out my back door with my keys, walk along the side of the house and get in the car. I hurry and am in the car right in front of him before he becomes aware of it. He was expecting me from the front and is shocked to realize what I am doing, and screams at me that he needs something from inside. I tell him that I will be right back. He kicks at my car and throws a bottle at it. I drive the two blocks to Eric's house and ask him to come home with me. When we arrive, Eric confronts Russell and tells him to leave. He becomes belligerent, so we call the police. Then, Russell leaves quickly.

 Drugs do terrible things to the people who use them and so much stealing and bodily harm result from this lifestyle. Destruction of families occurs nonstop with children or parents taking that first hit of what they think will allow a wondrous escape from reality. Prisons are full of druggies who, at times, revel in sharing their past offenses and how wonderful those times were. In their minds, they think the fellow inmates will look up to them, but they need to man up and admit their horrible wrong doing and ask forgiveness. Children are devalued and physical and mental child abuse is the norm in countless homes. Many give up caring for children that they love. Drug use is the priority and prostitution and robbery provide the funds for many.

What can these people do? I know that Christ is the answer. Christ is the answer! Christ is the answer! Move close to Him.

It is rare for me to get a good nights' sleep. Our home is almost 100 years old, and I hear many noises. They may not have bothered me in the past, but now they do because many thieves have been in and outside of our home as guests of Russell. One, in particular cased our home on a visit. He had been in prison for robbery two times, so I was very suspicious, and he wanted to go with Russell all through the house. I advised him to keep his seat! Finally, my concerns led us to the purchase of a security system. It does comfort me with so many crimes in our area.

Surprisingly, Russell is still working at the job he began when he was first released from jail. His paycheck is gone before he gets it. Banks and loan institutions know how to offer money for huge profits from payday to payday. I feel that what they do is a crime. It may not matter when the person is a drug user, but it does matter to people struggling on a low income. The percentage of profit on the money until payday loans is off the charts. I have a neighbor who struggles to make ends meet. Her water pipe recently developed a bad leak and she had no means to pay for the repair. She received a loan from one of these quick money establishments. Now, she is agonizing on how to repay it with the exorbitant interest rate. Her income does not cover her regular expenses, much less emergencies. Just this evening I made a small donation to help, but that really is not the solution. How can anyone with a conscience work for one of these places?

The values of many have sunk very low for the almighty dollar and for drug use. Russell borrowed from these places nonstop, and stayed a month or more behind on his paycheck. He needed money, money, money. He still loves to have it and to show it. Thousands of dollars were at his disposal when he was doing drugs, and as he tells me this, his face and gorgeous smile appear in memory of his money supply. Joy?

Many days I rise early and leave home before Russell's arrival, so that I can avoid being tormented with his needs. By the end of

September we decide to have him rent an apartment, so he will have a place to live and to alleviate his visits to us. We agree to pay the deposit and first month's rent for a total of $1000.00, and he will pay us back from his weekly pay checks. What were we thinking?

Things only get worse. I take pride in providing a decent place for him to live. We furnish it with a spare bed and linens. We find kitchens supplies and purchase many items that are required to be on your own. He lives there...for a while. He is getting into trouble with many people. He actually hocked the scooter that we purchased for his ride to work. Fortunately, we were able to pay $100 to the person who had it, and it was returned. Now, it is off limits to him, despite all his pleading to be allowed to use it. He has stolen from everyone he knows and many he doesn't, and they are out to get him. He is afraid to stay in his apartment because his enemies look for him there.

On Saturday evening October 13, 2012 he visits Shawna while Eric is not at home. She is glad to see him, but when she leaves the room, he is gone in a flash. He has taken the container of money that is on the kitchen counter. Change is added to it daily for their daughter's bank account and their estimate is that it contains about $300.00. Russell never had a better friend than Shawna. She was always happy for him to stay with her and Eric and consistently believed in him. When we all voiced concerns about his behavior, she was his staunch supporter. Now, she has been stepped on, chewed into tiny pieces and spit in the face by this robbery, and Eric feels the same. His nephew has pierced his heart and the worst is yet to come.

The following day, by phone, Russell and Eric discuss the theft. For some reason, Russell has often felt that if he screams and shouts loud enough, and often enough, and denies doing a bad deed over and over and over he will be believed. He even convinces himself of his innocence in the process. This is what he did on the phone with Eric. Then, Russell turns into his Dad, the Incredible Hulk, a totally different person who punches people to prove his point.

Finally, they agree to meet in the nearby bank parking lot. Eric has a friend go with him, as does Russell. We are horribly shocked by their confrontation. Russell has taken a heavy ax handle as a weapon and uses it to bludgeon Eric's head and arm. I am in shock over this attack! Eric's friend assists him, and he returns home with pain and anger. He thinks that his arm is broken, but delays a hospital visit. The following day, he stays home from work trying to heal physically and mentally. Russell goes to the ER complaining that his ribs may be broken, but he is fine. He probably saw the hospital visit as a possibility for pain medicine.

The next day, Doug has a deep discussion with Russell, and he says that he will seek drug treatment on the weekend. For now, he wants to keep his job. Same ole, same ole, same ole--come the weekend.

I have emailed our family the events of October 13-14 and, once again, requested many prayers. Doug's sister, Betse, responds eloquently: "In the dark of night, I get a lot of praying done--just picturing our family--and who has been hurt--and trying to plea for their protection, good, and ongoing closeness to God. I do hope that Russell will recognize that it's time to end this downward spiral of addiction. Everyone wants Russell to quit drugs, and quit preying on/attacking his closest loved ones. It will take a miracle, indeed, and we know he can't do it on his own, so the need for God is huge. May God's strength empower you to get through this crises...he is not taking responsibility for his own actions and is in deep denial about his behavior. If he can't stop, or get treatment, it's just a matter of time until he's locked up. I'll go back to praying."

Russell has no plans for drug rehab. By the last of October, in an effort to put an end to the menacing evil caused by drugs, Eric files assault and robbery charges against Russell. Now, he is nowhere to be found and has gone into hiding to escape being arrested. Soon, though, he reappears with his usual requests, and while the police can't locate him, we see or hear from him regularly. Often, he visits his Mom at the hospital where she works knowing that she will give him money as a bribe for him to leave. He is an embarrassment to her, and his previous visit was dramatic with him looking, full-fledged, like the druggie he is. Skinny, eyes squinty and dull, filthy clothing and a bad odor characterize him. He had actually slept under our outside deck on a cold night in November. That was his hiding place, unknown to us, until I glimpsed him in the back alley and became suspicious.

His apartment served him and us for less than one month, but was rented for two. We forfeited our deposit and all the articles purchased for his use there. When we cancelled the rent, someone else was already living there and had to be evicted. Another druggie said that he was taking care of it for Russell. The landlord said the place was an unbelievable mess, but she used our deposit money to have it cleaned. Two thousand dollars total for what we thought was our peace of mind down the drain. When will we learn our lesson? We have needs, but helping Russell has been a priority. We love our grandson and did everything we could to help him, but drugs show no mercy.

It appears that we, like Russell, have to learn our lesson the hard way. By mid November, we are once again robbery victims. He has taken a large tool box from the back of Doug's truck. Neighbors saw him, but didn't realize what he was doing. This has crushed Doug to the core with several thousand dollars of prized tools, some rare and irreplaceable, gone forever. They were tools that he has used for years and years and knew just which one was perfect for every job. Our hearts ache as we call the police to report this crime. And, our hearts ache because the thief is our grandson.

We are talking to God a lot these days, and we are requesting many prayers. Russell is a never ending story. His life reminds me of the movie Groundhog Day. I enjoy that movie, but not the way in which it applies to us. It hurts so bad to love a child this much and know what torment they are in. How can drugs take over so completely? What is the solution? What can be done? I am turning this over to The Lord, but the hurt encompasses me.

My tears are nonstop. Once again, my heart breaks. I know that Russell's addiction has meaning, but I have trouble dealing with it. He has certainly brought me a long way in my pursuit of a Christian life! I want his wonderful smile and sweetness. Drugs have taken that, and I know that I am not alone. I mourn for so many. What is important in life? Is it what money can buy? Is it your next fix? The solution is Jesus Christ! I love Him with all of my heart, yet many times, I short change Him with my time and faithfulness. Yes, this heartache does bring me closer to Him.

Beth has just called from the hospital where she works. Russell is there asking for food. She says that he admits to injecting drugs and that he slept outside last night. He is dirty and smelly. What can anyone do? We can and do pray. Russell is a fortunate child to have his mother's prayers and so many more. I believe that Russell will be with me in heaven one day. God does love me that much, but Russell's journey there may be hard. I have to let it go.

I email our family on November 21, 2012: just a quick note to let you know that Russell is in jail as of Nov. 20. We are relieved and don't know how long they can keep him. I would be happy for him to be put away for a very long time! Again, he misses Thanksgiving and Christmas celebrations with family. Doug and I, and the rest of the family want nothing to do with him.

Groundhog Day! I found in my journal notes that Doug and I saw the movie Groundhog Day on March 6, 1993. Bill Murray is fabulous in this role! I have watched it countless times! We loved the movie, but detest the similarity to the series of events in our lives, over and over.

Notes 15
(Beth's Letters)

November 30, 2012

Russell,

    I am writing to let you know that I am thinking about you while you are in this situation again. Yes, I lied to you about what I would do when you went to jail, and I don't feel bad about that at all. You have basically destroyed your family by being so greedy for money, drugs and the life you want to live where you can party and act like a pimp. You always seem to think that your actions have no consequences, and that somehow you are never to blame for anything that you do to hurt others. In your mind, it is always someone else's fault. I don't even know if you can begin to understand the hurt you have caused your family, maybe you don't really care...that is what it feels like to all of us. I don't know what you want or expect from any of us after this, but you need to understand... it's up to you this time. People are not going to trust you or give you more chances when you burn them so badly. Don't get me wrong, you are still loved. The only help any of us can give you is our prayers. Maybe you think that's not much, but that's worth more than anything else if you believe, and pray also. God will make any situation better. Now is the time for you to turn to God, and pray with all your might to help you turn your life around and be able to stay away from all the demons that drag you down and ruin your life. You are so young...you have time to have a great life. You could be an inspiration to people who have had problems like you. Your personality can shine like the sun when you are on the right track. We have all said that you could be an awesome car salesman, but why do that when you could change people's lives by telling them your story, and about how God can make changes that seem impossible.

In the past couple of weeks, two young people I know lost their lives. I'm telling you this because these two people had great lives, they each had so much to look forward to, and drugs were not a part of their life. The first who passed was a girl only thirty, who recently finished college with a double major in engineering and architecture. She was very smart, had a wonderful family, was engaged to be married, but was diagnosed with breast cancer in March 2012. Her cancer spread fast, she was very ill the past couple of months, and died last week. The second was a thirty-five year old coach. He was loved by all his students, his team, his church (he was a youth leader), his family, and he had so many friends.

Everyone who knew him had something good to say about him. He died unexpectedly in his sleep. He was healthy, with no history of any health problems. He had a wife, a three year old daughter, and an eight month old son. His funeral is Tuesday and will most likely have more people than this town has seen for a long time, if ever. Again, I'm telling you this because I feel like you are wasting your life. These two people had great lives, and they didn't get a chance to move forward, and grow, and do more, and get better, and help others. You can do great things...don't waste your life. You never know when you won't have another chance. Put God first and you can expect great things! As I have told you before, I think Teen Challenge is the way for you to get your life back. You have to contact them, but it's up to you.

December 30, 2012

Russell,

   Well, you just tried to call me again, but I'm not ready to talk to you just yet. If you want to communicate with me, you will have to do it through a letter. You should send it to Granny's house because sometimes I don't get our mail (it gets lost or stolen).
   I am wondering what you are thinking and doing while you're in jail this time. Last time, I know you lied to me a lot about the whole girlfriend situation, telling me your family was most important to you, but she was the main

thing on your mind. I really WANTED to believe you. I was hoping that FINALLY you realized your family is the most important thing in your life. WE have been there for you, trying to help you through all your difficult times. Trying different ways to help you get your life on the right track, but it's never been enough for you. Friends, girlfriends, and partying have always taken top priority in your life. I have always felt like the bad guy to you. It seems that no matter how hard I try to steer you in a certain direction, you would tell me I was stupid, or I had it all wrong, that you're a grown man, you could decide your own life. Even when you were younger you would tell me I was crazy, stupid, too strict, just plain wrong. I've always known it would be very hard to keep you on a good path. I knew you were capable, because there were times in your life when you did SO well. But for some reason, I guess maybe, genetics, you were always drawn to the bad things. When you lived at home, I did my very best to keep you from venturing down the wrong path, but once you left, I knew there would be loads of trouble before you would (hopefully) come to your senses and realize your family has always wanted what's best for you. I knew you would have to make mistakes and get in some trouble before you would see what you really needed to do with your life. I keep holding my breath hoping you will have that "aha" moment. The moment you realize life isn't all about what you want...life is about living the best life you can, so you can represent the gifts God has given you. You don't get to live just for fun.

That's not why He gave us life. He does allow us to have fun, but we have to respect Him by living like He wants us to. No person on this earth is perfect. We all have a different path. We all sin in different ways. But there is NO WAY to have a good life without GOD!

My heart hurts, and I feel sick to my stomach when I start thinking about you. I want SO much for you to have a good life and be a part of our family. But I have realized that no matter how bad I want that, it doesn't matter unless you want it too. I can't help you, I can't do it for you, and neither can anyone else. We all have done all we can to help you. You have to fix your life and your relationships on your own. You are, as you like to say, "a grown man," so now it's up to you. Your family loves you, and we all pray for you. You can accomplish ANYTHING through GOD! I have seen miracles, and I have had miracles in my own life, so I have NO DOUBT! If you truly will pray and trust, with all your heart, GOD will heal everything and give you another chance at a good life. You are so young, don't give up. You could have an amazing journey ahead of you.

When I start writing, I don't want to stop. I keep thinking of more and more things I want to say. I know it's probably best to send little bits at a time rather than bombard you with everything I have on my mind. I want you to really think about what I have said and take it to heart. Just as I have always tried to do...I am trying to steer you back in the right direction. I am your Mother, and I love you with all my heart. I want you to have a good life.

Mary Feuchtenberger

I put all my faith in God knowing that He can rescue you, but you have to try.

   PRAY, PRAY, PRAY, BELIEVE, BELIEVE, and BELIEVE...GOD SENT HIS ONLY SON TO DIE FOR OUR SINS...HE LOVES US!!!

Faith, Hope, Love

PS-Kylie loves the cross.
She made it into a necklace and wears it all the time.

January 27, 2013

Russell,

   I'm sure you're wondering why you haven't heard from me in so long. Honestly, I've thought about writing and sending money, but suddenly I remember how you treated me while you were out last time, and the time before, and after Mountaineer Challenge Academy, and always really.
   I feel like God is reminding me that you've had so many chances and that now it's up to you. It's up to you to surrender to God and know that your life will never get better without Him. You need to go through hard times because you've had so many opportunities to do well in your life, but you always choose the wrong path. Nobody can make your decisions; nobody can make your life easy now. Your easy days are over.
   I don't know where you will go if they just let you out of jail like they did last time. No

one in your family will take you in this time. Although, we all love you and pray for you, we cannot trust you. You have only proven to hurt those you supposedly love. For some reason, your friends/girlfriends have always come first. Your family has been the ones to turn to when you need something. It feels like you think that is all we are supposed to do...just help you with whatever your problem is...like you have no feelings for us, you just know where to go when you need money, food, a ride, a place to stay...

I am blessed to be so busy, I can hardly think about what you've done or what will happen when you get out. Haley is getting ready to go to college; Kylie and Kendra have horse lessons and gymnastics, as well as school related stuff. My work keeps me very busy, and then, of course, all of the regular stuff at home (cooking, cleaning, laundry, etc). I do pray for you often, and I truly hope you can get your life on the right track. I feel in my heart that one day you will get straightened out...I just don't know when. I do know that no one else can do it for you. It's a big job with a lot of work ahead of you, but I know you can do it! Just remember Phil. 4:13 All things are possible through God who strengthens me.

Those words are so true!!!! I've been through a lot in my life. I've made mistakes, gotten off track, but God forgives. He guides, and He loves us. He wants us to be happy and to do well in this life on earth. One thing to keep in mind is that this life on earth is not all that there is. Heaven awaits us, and that is our reward for dealing with the hardships of this life.

Mary Feuchtenberger

There are so many stories in the Bible about people who were true servants of God, but they still suffered through terrible things. You just have to keep in your mind that God will see you through, no matter how hopeless your situation seems. He will never leave you. When you feel like He isn't there, pray, ask Him to let you know He is with you. This may be your opportunity to know God better than anyone. Who knows what can await you if you truly surrender your life to Him?

I love you, and I have faith in you. Mom

Notes 16
(Change)

Russell is calling from Southern Regional Jail, but we do not answer. He writes several letters trying to explain his actions. Basically, he says that all he cared about was getting a pill, and that he would go days without bathing and changing clothes because nothing mattered. He has learned the hard way that he can't live in Princeton when he gets out of jail, and hopefully, he has learned that God is the only way to live the right kind of life. Now, he would like to go locally to Teen Challenge drug rehab and swears there will be no more problems, and he asks forgiveness. His hopes are to be released from jail with Eric dropping charges, so he can do drug rehab.

However, felony charges cannot and should not be dropped. Russell needs enforcement to stay away from drugs. He asks that I send a study Bible, one that he can understand. He has made a small cross in prison and sends it to Kylie. She is delighted with a gift from this brother whom she loves. He writes "hope you all have a good Christmas and "Please write back soon."

Mary Feuchtenberger

I write him a very brief note.

```
Dear Russell,

   I am writing to let you know that I do love
you. Because I love you, your life choices
hurt and stress me. I do not plan on writing
you again. We are worn out with trying to
help you and worrying over your needs. As I
always say: prayer is the answer, but you have
to want The Lord instead of the bad stuff. I
hope that you can get your life back on the
right track.

Love Granny
```

    Finally, I begin sending some scripture that I print on cards. A favorite verse is from (NIV) Isaiah 40:31 "**But those who hope in The Lord will renew their strength. They will soar on wings like eagles; they will run and not grow weary, they will walk and not be faint.**"

    Once again, we have peace of mind. Jail is a good place for him and for us, but jail is not really the answer. It is just a temporary solution, with people together for similar crimes, putting in time day after day. I am a person with a lot of empathy, so I understand another person's feelings and sympathize with them. Prison is an unimaginable place to have to endure, and for those incarcerated long periods or for life, it is horrid to think of. Surely, many can turn their focus to God and find comfort in the realization of how wonderful their next life will be. Russell's imprisonment certainly works wonders for my seeking God. What does it take for you?

    As we begin the New Year, Russell meets with his lawyer, but no decisions are made. Later, he pleads guilty to a felony, but has not been sentenced. Beth is busy trying to have him put in a long term drug rehab rather than jail. She has talked with a friend who knows of a Christian drug rehab in Texas and highly recommends it, plus the price seems doable. Now, the problem is to have the lawyers and judge in agreement. By March, she has talked with the director of the program, and he has a place for Russell. It is surprising to learn that one man is there from our small town of Princeton.

Plans are put in motion, and Russell is released to Beth's and my custody on March 28. Much has to be done in a short time. He is required to have a photo ID for the plane ticket to Texas. Amazingly, we locate his birth certificate and required papers just before closing time at the DMV. Then, a plane ticket is purchased online for the next day with departure at an airport 100 miles from here. Shopping has to be done for clothing needs and toilet items, and his suitcase needs to be ready for early morning departure. We know that the Lord made these provisions for us, with so many variables coming into place in a brief time.

Russell is spending the night in our home, yet Doug has not looked at or spoken to him and won't for months to come. Forgiveness can be difficult. But, the most difficult part for me is just seeing and talking with him. I have agreed to take him to the airport and we are up at 4:00 am, because he can't sleep and we need to leave by 6:00 am. My heart is aching. We have some good time together, and I do see his beautiful smile through the uncertainty and sadness. We discuss his worries and his hopes for the future.

I write my cousin Sandra the following letter on March 30, 2013:

> I am in so much pain from spending time with Russell. He stayed here Thursday night, and I took him to the Roanoke airport Friday. He was released from jail Thursday and looked awful. He was very thin and said he doesn't feel good and thinks he may have some druggie disease. He was in jail for a little over 4 months and that may be part of it. I wish that we could have had his health checked, but no time for

that. He was very hyper, but had calmed a little by Friday. I saw some of his sweetness, and it has just broken my heart so much that I am a crying wreck. He has hurt the family horribly. We will have no contact for a month. Certainly, there is a lot of hope and faith in answers to prayers. It has been unbelievably hard on me.

We have no Easter plans. I may crawl in a hole. Eric took a mini vacation, and Beth is going to her in-laws. Sorry to distribute my sadness. I know that you have plenty of that, and I do still know that God is good. Hugs, Mary.

I post a photo of Russell from his better days, and a friend responds telling me that I have a handsome grandson. I respond to her: "Thank you for the comment on my grandson. He doesn't look nearly so handsome now. He is a druggie, and I put him on a plane yesterday for a one year drug rehab in Texas. I would appreciate prayers." It is wonderful to have friends who pray, and I am grateful to Facebook for providing the connection.

Thank you God for another chance! This post from The Purpose Driven Life applies to us and to many and is welcoming advice. "God's love is everlasting, and his patience endures forever. If you have to cry out for God's help two hundred times a day to defeat a particular temptation, He will still be eager to give mercy and grace, so come boldly. Ask Him for the power to do the right thing and then expect Him to provide it." Thank you, thank you, God, for so many blessings!

I am thinking of all the ways we tried to make Russell happy in the past, and very much of it is by providing material goods. Kids feel entitled to brand name everything, regardless of the costs. Often we agree with them because so and so said so. I don't know how to get that misconception out of our minds. I do know that I get a thrill by purchasing from flea markets and yard sales. My porch furniture for many years was second hand and better than new, as is much of our furniture today. When Beth was a young teen, Eric bought her crystal earrings that looked like diamonds from a discount shop for one dollar. They were good looking and friends asked if they were "real." I said "yes, they are real."

Notes 17

(Recreation)

Comparing what you have materially to what others have is a poor way to determine your needs. Television advertising and other media ads prompt us to make unnecessary purchases. Timothy 1:6-10 (NIV) **"But godliness with contentment is great gain. For we brought nothing into the world, and take nothing out of it. But if we have food and clothing, we will be content with that. Those who want to get rich fall into temptation and a trap and into many foolish desires that plunge people into ruin and destruction. For the love of money is a root of all kinds of evil. Some people, eager for money, have wandered from the faith and pierced themselves with many griefs."**

Russell, along with many of us, (myself included), focuses too much on what money can buy. He makes his love of money known. Much of the time it could only purchase drugs. What can it purchase for you? Food for the hungry, fresh water in barren countries, clothing for the poor, medicine, protection, support for the church? My understanding is that those with more money than their needs are given the excess so that they may share and help others. Admittedly, fiscal fitness is needed, but enjoy God's blessings without the love of the money.

My advice to Russell and his friends and others is to make a conscious effort to use what God has provided. WV and most states have an overflowing abundance of things to enjoy. You may be surprised to learn of the rewards of church attendance. Pastors Gary, Bill and Chris have all heaped blessings on those in attendance at First Christian Church. Members really do become a family that cares for one another, and worship brings joy and peace throughout the week. Countless activities provide fellowship: Bible study, choir, vespers, family dinners, circle meetings, church travel and much more. And believe it or not, a funeral can be a fabulous celebration and joyous coming together...and a true blessing. What will your funeral be?

Explore your state! WV is rich with mountains and rivers. Fishing, swimming, water and snow sports abound! Many people in WV enjoy the sport of hunting. Years ago, Kathy, a teacher friend shared a story of her husband and friends preparing to take a camper to go hunting for a few days. She said that they packed all sorts of snacks and food and drinks. They gathered reading materials, possibly including a few risqué magazines. Several games were included and lots of warm clothing. Sleeping bags, a heater and flashlights were packed. Her husband said, that, when they prepared to return from the trip, he was upset that he could not find his gun, but later realized that he had forgotten to take it!

Get a membership in a gym. We have a top of the line fitness center in Princeton. Participate in sports or watch sports. Car racing is the main event in our household. My husband and son both enjoy dirt track racing at Princeton Speedway. Some, like my brother-in-law John, love to refurbish antique cars and drive them in parades and various events. The Princeton Rays baseball team has games locally and travel to nearby towns, and welcome your attendance. Golf is certainly prevalent in WV and most everywhere and provides hours of entertainment. Schools have numerous sports and music events and more. In my youth, I enjoyed tennis and my father-in-law and others played in their 60's and 70's. Bowling is enjoyable for all ages. At one time, I liked the card game of bridge and know the fun and difficulties of duplicate bridge. As I am watching TV, I see that some people enjoy marble playing.

Mary Feuchtenberger

The lake has given us and our family and friends countless hours of entertainment. We love that Todd and Ginger shared their dock and boat with us and that we developed a close bond because of lake time. Just this past week, Doug had to prove that he could still ski… at age 70, so Todd took him out as a storm began with HEAVY rain. I swear that I heard thunder, but he couldn't be deterred as he slalomed all over that lake! God is good, all of the time! No one enjoys the water more than Betse and I. We will both agree to "jump in the lake" at a moments' notice! We enjoy the wildlife there, especially the herons. Yet, one time as Betse was swimming, a blue heron decided that she might make a good meal! They are huge birds, and it circled several times watching her head and odd looking gloves paddling in the water…lunch! Thankfully, it changed its' mind, just as it seemed ready to scoop her up. Life is an adventure and we share its' joys! We actually see few lake swimmers, but many boaters. Some lake campers can be found playing horseshoes and, of course, corn hole!

Give your time to help someone. Often a visit can brighten your day as well as that of someone else. Our church has mission teams who travel to work for others, and they praise God for the blessings that they receive. Reading, movie attendance and eating out are enjoyable recreation. One evening of dining out on St. Patrick's Day stays in my mind. The servers at the restaurant were dressed and painted in all green, and noise makers and hats were given to diners. The roasted duck that I ordered was delicious and at meal's end, I was pleased to receive a small cake that seemed to be covered with coconut. It was hard to tell in the darkened restaurant. I hadn't ordered it, but assumed that it was a freebie that I would share with my dining companion, Brenda. Imagine my surprise, and then laughter, as I tried to cut into it and found that it was a rolled up wet washcloth for me to use to clean my hands!

While sewing used to be a life necessity, many people today think of it as a fabulous form of entertainment. Television programs feature fashion designers being judged on their garments and receiving high paying jobs in the clothing industry. Other people enjoy making quilts or doing needlework for recreation. I have a special sampler given to me by my friend Tom, who said that cross stitching was a stress reliever. Many friends love to quilt, as did women years ago. When my grandmother lost a daughter at the age of five, she took her dresses and made them into a quilt. I cannot imagine how many tears went into that precious creation. I am honored to have and display it in my home. Quilt shows and judging are a part of most state fairs and provide joy to many.

Traveling is almost always wonderful entertainment. I read, with envy, of the travels of Tom and Janie, just today, on their way to Paris. Doug and I enjoy our drives within the United States and recommend many state and national parks. One, and maybe more, of my former students makes parachute jumps…sounds very fascinating. I see by Adam's posts that he goes to air shows, museums, kayaks and may be taking piloting lessons. Whew! His activities wear me out, but such a good example of living life to the fullest in the right way.

I saw a 70 year old man on TV yesterday, and he was flying through the air. Hang gliding looked dangerous, but fulfilled his need for sport. Bridge Day is celebrated at New River Gorge Bridge (one of the world's largest arch suspension bridges) just a short distance from here with many taking the plunge via a special parachute, but just watching can be fun. Zip lining and tubing are offered at nearby parks. White water rafting invites locals and tourists to participate. West Virginia is amazing in its' beauty and is equal to or better than any nationally advertised spot on earth. Many natural highs can be enjoyed in this foremost state of God's creation!

One of the biggest flea markets in the US occurs in Hillsville VA, just an hour's drive from here, and many smaller flea markets flourish throughout the year. The Chuck Mathena Center is a beautiful theatre that offers fabulous events to the public and is located in Princeton. Coal mines and caves can be explored, and beautiful arts and crafts are sold at Tamarack and other tourist stops and shops. Some groups do Civil War and Revolutionary War reenactments. The town of Bramwell, WV offers home tours and wine tasting events, theatre and much more with restaurants, fine foods and shops.

Recently, a trail nearby was opened for bikers, along with places for them to stay and a highly rated restaurant. Waterfalls can be enjoyed just a short distance away and camping is available in several areas. WV has many beautiful parks to enjoy, with Pipestem State Park just a short distance from Princeton. A fiddlers' convention was just advertised on television and sounds like fun with blue grass and country music and hymns on Sunday.

Volunteers are needed at hospitals and animals shelters and countless other places. For me, being in or near the water is the best of the best! Formulate healthy entertainment. There is much of it in or near southern WV. Focus on the good, and I quote John Wesley. "Do all the good you can. By all the means you can. In all the ways you can. In all the places you can. At all the times you can. To all the people you can, as long as ever you can."

It is difficult to understand, when reviewing the richness of our area, the deluge of drug use. It is hurtful to find an article by a former drug abuser and prostitute in our newspaper, the Bluefield Daily Telegraph dated May 26, 2013. Her description of Princeton, WV is sad. She first came to Princeton twenty years ago and left in 2002. She says, "What I discovered there was a drug culture that paled in comparison to any other I have ever seen to this day." Her feeling was that prostitution had become part of the culture. She encountered violence and was robbed, raped and beaten in our area and knew women who were murdered. She, unknowingly, lived with a murderer. She realizes that many see trashiness and the bad in street people and prostitutes, but cautions, that beneath the visible may well be a person "literally dying to get out."

I, myself, have been guilty of judging these people. I found this message on social media. Sometimes the nicest people you meet are covered in tattoos and sometimes the most judgmental people you meet go to church on Sundays. Again, prayer is the answer. Pray without ceasing! Think about their needs and ask God to help them. Until, I read this former prostitute's letter, I had never prayed for these street people. Disgust is what I felt when I saw them, yet we can and should be a missionary in our own town. Pray for them!

Upon leaving Princeton for Tennessee she was arrested and spent 7 months in jail. From there she went to a 28 day in-patient drug rehab and then to a halfway house for a year. She attended AA/Narcotics Anonymous meetings and was court ordered to enroll in college classes. She now says she called on a higher power and is "a daughter of a loving God." Her life is on track with a college major in human services and her hope is for others like her to be given opportunities for reform. We know all things are possible, only believe. With arms wide open he'll welcome you. These words are from the hymn It Is No Secret written by Stuart Hamblen. I find them very comforting.

The chimes of time ring out the news another day is through. Someone slipped and fell, was that someone you? ... Do not be disheartened, for I have news for you. It is no secret what God can do. What He's done for others, He'll do for you.

Wikipedia information says that the hymn writer, Stuart Hamblen, was a well known song writer and personality in Hollywood in the 1950's. He is described as a person who drank and partied too much. One evening, he attended a tent revival and believed that the preacher was talking about him in his message. He felt a burden and later went to the pastor and asked for prayer. He was told to pray to God and was saved. Later a friend asked if it was worth it to give up his bad habits, since it was a struggle and his answer was "yes." His friend said he didn't understand how he could do it so easily and Stuart said, "It's no big secret. All things are possible with God." His friend said that he should write a song about it and he did! It turns out the pastor was Billy Graham and the friend was John Wayne.

Hymns can be very uplifting, and God loves for us to sing them. Have you been to church and heard that favorite song from childhood? The feeling it conveys is priceless. Sometimes hearing one brings a huge smile for me and other times, tears dampen my cheeks. Hymns are another one of our blessings to enjoy free of charge.

Notes 18
(Rehab)

Russell makes it safely to the Texas drug rehab facility. The director calls to let us know and to remind us that there will be no communication for a month. After that, there is an occasional call. It is wonderful to know that he is 1500 miles away in a Christian environment, and we are grateful to our Heavenly Father. As far as I know, this rehab is different from many. It has less than 10 men in the program, and the majority of the time is spent working and in church or Bible study. It sounds fabulous to me! Russell has a few requests that we honor, but the director prefers that he does without the material things he has requested, and that is probably best.

Russell is very unhappy upon his arrival in Texas. His first airplane flight left him fearful of ever flying again! The plane was crowded, had some turbulence, and with a layover in Chicago, he was uneasy about making connections. Plus, he was just out of jail and in poor health with many uncertainties. He was exchanging one prison for another and missed his jail buddies and routine. He preferred Southern Regional Jail to the limitations first imposed in rehab, and it took several months for him to comply. He had gotten away with tobacco use in prison and now was having nicotine withdrawal. Manual labor was a requirement, and hard for him since he hadn't done physical work for several months. I say the more hard work, the better the outcome!

He became a whiny baby requesting a return to WV and arguing with the rehab director who stood his ground in denial. However, at one point the director called and discussed the difficulty in keeping Russell and the possibility of returning him to prison. He was one hard headed young man, and his stubbornness slowed improvement. The indication was that Russell was the first person this facility could not help. Again and again, we petitioned our heavenly Father for what is best for Russell. We did not know, but put it in God's hands.

On July 11, I write Russell a letter. "I want to remind you Russell, that everything in life is not fair. Many times you mention when you get upset with someone, that it isn't fair. John the Baptist, the man who actually baptized Jesus had his head cut off. Was that fair? You have had many advantages that other people haven't had. Try not to look at the bad, but look at the good. Don't blame others for things that happen. The result of many bad things is for you to turn to God and accept it. My Mother was a wonderful Christian woman, yet she was blind for much of her life...not very fair, but she did not complain. She accepted it. I know that you love money and what it can buy, but you need to focus on other things. Family and friends are extremely important. You can turn your life around if you choose to, through God. According to the Bible, not many of us are going to heaven. It is hard for us to give up sin and trust The Lord. Pappy and I have many blessings since we have made Christ and the church the main focus of our life. It is possibly harder at your age, but if you accept Him you can have many rewards now! The best reward is a personal relationship with Christ! He brings amazing peace and joy into your whole life! I feel that

Mary Feuchtenberger

we will not be willing to help you much longer if you continue to stray from what is right. Many things besides drugs are bad, so try to eliminate other sinful acts. Then, you may need training before getting a job. Foremost is to love God and one another. The only way through all of this is Jesus Christ! I love you and want only the best for you. I pray for you and every person there. XO Granny.

Finally, the director called to convey that Russell is doing better. He has been there for three months. Some drug programs do not last nearly that long, but Russell is scheduled for a year. Thank you Lord!

I soon receive a marvelous post that brings tears. "July 21, 2013 got saved granny so u know" and he calls to confirm his message. "I didn't want to walk up there Granny, but I had to." He said that the pastor talked about Daniel and the lion's den and said how God had helped Daniel to even sleep with the lions. It wasn't Daniel's friends or family that helped; it was God! Russell said he knew that was true, so he had to walk up and accept Christ as his Savior! He says that he feels so much better now! Victory in Jesus, this hymn, composed by Eugene Bartlett, speaks for many who defeat the burdens of sin.

I heard an old, old story, how a Savior came to glory, how He gave His life on Calvary to save a wretch like me; I heard about His groaning of His precious blood's atoning, then I repented of my sins and won the Victory. O victory in Jesus, my Savior, forever, He sought me and bought me with His redeeming love;

Many people see Russell's post and offer encouraging words-"what an awesome answer to prayer!"-"I am proud of you Russell! Love and hugs!" "Love u Russell, God is good." So proud and happy for you. God is AWESOME!! "I'm proud of you bubby. I love you." I write, "I am praising The Lord for the great things I am hearing about you!" 2 Corinthians 5 HCSB. **"Therefore, if anyone is in Christ, he is a new creation; old things have passed away,**

and look, new things have come." I'm looking forward to this new creation!

He posts that "I have been in little trouble here but I'm done getting in trouble; things are going to be fine just want u all to know I have been putting things in God's hands and he took a lot of my problems away. I am very thankful for that...love u all."

Later; "things couldn't be better so glad God is working out all my problems...VERY BLESSED. His Mamaw Jan posts, "love you Russell. God is good!" His Mom, "So proud and happy for you. God is AWESOME!"

Notes 19
(Cousins)

I am taking a break from Russell this week, since Sandra and Connie, my first cousins, are visiting. I am blessed to have them, and honored that they would take the time to travel to our home. I pick them up at the Roanoke VA airport, and we enjoy God's nature on our way to Princeton. The beauty of the mountains is outstanding, driving from Virginia to West Virginia with mist drifting through sunlight and fifty shades of green on the summertime trees. Those who haven't visited Wild and Wonderful West Virginia, have something to add to your bucket list.

My cousin's description of her trip may entice you: "home again, home again, jiggity jog. I had a wonderful trip to VA/WV with cousins and sister. Ah, the mountains, the luscious food prepared by a cook extraordinaire, fresh everything, Doug's wine club samples, visits to old and new haunts (cemeteries and abandoned amusement park!), thousands of Boy Scouts and their leaders who were winding down their jamboree in the new multimillion dollar facility, thoughts about bungee jumping and rafting at New River Gorge. Maybe when I am 80. Exciting visit with my 96 year old uncle, who told a great story about an old relative who claimed he could fight a damn Yankee with a corn stalk? Thank you...for insisting that I make the trip to Almost Heaven!"

Groundhog Day in West Virginia

We had afternoons of delight plus mornings and evenings of sheer pleasure in one another's company. We traveled a short distance to Lake Shawnee where we swam as kids. It is now a deserted, eerie looking amusement park, and also home to Native American burial grounds. Some say it is haunted, and paranormal activity has been recorded there with movement of empty, rusty swings and sounds of absent children's laughter. The area may be explored on special evenings in October as part of Halloween festivities and ghost hunting.

We journeyed to New River Gorge and chatted with several scouts who were ending their 2013 Jamboree. WV received many accolades from tourists who thoroughly enjoyed their holiday. You will be amazed at the beauty of WV here and may take a fabulous walk just below the bridge to receive a tremendous view of nature at its' finest!

Bluefield WV is advertised as natures air conditioned city and it is! While summer temperatures are hot, it seldom reaches 90 degrees, and if it does the city serves free lemonade. We visit John and Betse's home in Bluefield, since it is always a delight to see what new antique treasure that John has found and the home is outstanding in its' architecture. A video of it may be viewed on YouTube Hill House WV PBS.

One evening meal was especially delicious with gourmet dining and presentation at the Mountain Creek Restaurant of Pipestem State Park. A tram ride high above the grounds provided the transportation, and the mountainous landscape was amazing with a reconstructed moonshine still, hidden among the rocks and foliage.

Off the beaten path, Bramwell WV has amazing homes and scenery. We had a yummy lunch and fun exploring the quaint stores. A couple from our church, Tracy and Aaron, recently exchanged marriage vows with a Steampunk wedding theme in Bramwell. Their photos with period costumes, brick streets and lavish century old homes with lush landscaping would rival those of top designers! They need to be in a magazine and, hopefully, will be. If you time your arrival right, you may enjoy the musical, Smoke on the

Mary Feuchtenberger

Mountain, performed in the beautiful small <u>Wesleyan Church in Bramwell.</u> This is the perfect getaway off the beaten path in southern WV!

My cousins and I celebrated WV every minute and loved it. Tamarack is a great shopping jaunt with fine arts and crafts from all of WV. We saw award winning water color paintings from Rita, a Princeton artist, and the paintings of many others. Beautiful pottery, WV glass, marbles, handmade toys, handsome hand crafted furniture, fabulous jewelry, homemade sauces and sweets and more were amazing with fine dining by the Greenbrier Chefs.

The drive back to Princeton presented a view that I call the Four Seasons Grand Canyon. It is an unbelievable outpouring of God's bounty with magnificent mountains and trees and greenery as far as the eye can see. You will be amazed if you make the trip! We found that the western part of Virginia is also stunning as you travel to West Virginia with Big Walker and East River mountains having tunnels to travel through and then view the marvelous rolling hills and valleys and oceans of trees.

I realize that God bestowed our family this land to live in and enjoy each day of our lives. And, for our final resting place is a special cemetery reaching to the clouds in honor of those buried there. Upon entering the gate, there is an indescribable stillness in the air and fullness in the heart as we walk among the graves. The hymn, In the Garden, immediately resonates within this hallowed place. If you know this hymn, sing along as you read. Rejoice in our Lord! And it is always good to Google a hymn and to listen to many renditions of it. Joy comes from this salutation to God!

```
I come to the garden alone while the dew is
still on the roses And the voice I hear falling
on my ear The Son of God discloses And He walks
with me, and He talks with me, And He tells me
I am his own; And the joy we share as we tarry
there, None other has ever known. He speaks,
and the sound of His voice is so sweet the birds
```

hush their singing, And the melody that He gave to me within my heart is ringing

Many ancient tombstones speak of our history, and tears flow gently as we share memories. Again, my cousin writes eloquently of this family place and, also, pays tribute to our veterans: "I'm thinking about a little mountain-top cemetery in Elgood, WV, near my home town. My people's bones and ashes are there, as mine will be one of these days. My grandfather White was a veteran of some skirmish called the Philippine Insurrection. My great grandfather was once sheriff of Mingo County, WV, famous for those Hatfield's and McCoy's, so he was in a war zone of his own. Other veteran relatives are in cemeteries in the vicinity, the dearest of whom is Uncle Dave, a combatant on Guadalcanal in WWII. Gratitude to Herbert, the Doug's and my other vets who are still alive and kicking! Thank you to all these brave men in my past, and love to the women who stood and waited."

Regretfully, many have unpleasant memories of childhood cemetery and reunion trips on barely paved, winding roads that sickened us. Still, we desire to return when it is our time and to visit before our time, the peaceful hilltop with scenic pastoral images in the valley below. West Virginia has been called Almost Heaven and, also, Wild and Wonderful! Both are accurate. My cousin's husband vows not to return, after riding in the back seat to place a grave marker for the first time. Those crooked roads bring motion sickness, but for family hold priceless memories. We search out Gussie and Aunt Ine's home and Luther and Lottie's place and Aunt Teeny's. Tunny and Mody lived there too, and we wonder where on earth all of these odd family names came from? Even our grandparents names are not common---Bal and Mabel!

We laugh when we speak of using the outhouse at Elgood and, yes, there was an old catalog for toilet paper! It was the worst of the worst to have to occupy that smelly little outdoor building. We remember our dread of the drive, but our delight in being there. The church has grown in size and is special, for we recently used it to say goodbye to Jimmy and many others over the years. A large old school sits across from the church and was home and studio to a French artist a few years back. Boarded up is the country store that we begged for pennies to visit and entice our sweet tooth. The small, wooden, barn like, one room schoolhouse, still in Elgood, brings pride as we think of our grandfather who taught there over one hundred years ago and had as a student, the woman he later married, our grandmother.

Letters written by him during their courting days are a family treasure from the early 1900's. He was in the military and she was a young country girl. Parts of a letter postmarked Oct 25, 1913 from Recruiting Station Hinton WVa. to Miss Mabel Holdren Elgood, WVa.

"My Dear Mabel......I am most crazy to be up there to go to some of those apple peelings. Have you been to anymore? I bet there will be some dances. You remember the last one? At least that was my last one. I shall never forget; for I was swinging you for a partner, and you wanted to move from the head of the line so we wouldn't have to start first. If there is a big dance somewhere this fall or winter, I want to be present for certain. Will you let me know? ....the school boys and one of our teachers meet three nights each week for a glee club. Gee, we do some singing. "The Billy Goat" is one of our favorites and some more like it. The teachers say it puts new life in us. It looks like acting a dam fool I think. Though, I enjoy it very much.

There is a new kind of picture show making the rounds now; we had them here last night, for the first time. There is some class to them, I'll tell you. Also, had a carnival just closed two or three nights ago. I had more girls than I knew what to do with. My best one was red headed. I was afraid she might get angry. You know how red headed people are.

 How are you doing in school? I just look for you to get a whipping this winter.....I suppose someone has to go husk corn.....you wrote me such a short letter. I believe you are angry with me. Though, I am sorry to think so, for you are the bestest girl at Elgood, I think. .... if you do get out of being with me, I am going to put you in a mud hole the next time I see you. ...do you want me to ever go to Elgood again? I enjoyed being with you oh so much! I was almost ready to cry when I left, but I knew if I cried everybody would laugh at me. I don't think they should do you? I would like to take you down there (Norfolk) next fall and throw you in the sea. Would you like to go? I am sincerely, James B. White. Entertaining to read and hard to believe that my grandfather was 27 when he wrote this letter, and my grandmother was 17. Times quickly change!

Notes 20
(Texas)

Russell is suffering in the Texas heat. From time to time I search for the weather there, and while it has very good winter temperatures, the summer heat is hard to fathom. Many summer days that I search, it is close to or over 100 degrees. He complains a little, but deals with working there better than many. He is only 6 miles from Mexico in a very different environment from our four season city. Mostly, I learn of his activities from social media, and we message each other. Photos are posted of him at work cutting and trimming trees. Other photos show the rehab facility and friends from there.

Once again, he has missed a fabulous beach trip in the summer of 2013. It was truly a family affair that included Doug's brother, sister and niece as well as Eric and Beth and their families for a total of 14. Oceanfront with a pool, amazing weather, the best house ever and fabulous family fun…blessed! Russell also misses a few trips to the lake with us and Todd and Ginger. He used to enjoy it so much with water skiing, knee boarding and tubing. It is difficult to understand the lure of drugs compared to the lure of water.

From time to time in the fall of 2013, he longs for home and calls to express extreme sadness. My empathy clicks in, and I pray for his comfort. His court date isn't until March of 2014 when he completes rehab. However, the other man from Princeton has a December court date, and plans are being made for the rehab director to drive

Groundhog Day in West Virginia

to Princeton for that, so we offer finances for the trip with Russell accompanying them. Still, we communicate little, so I will share what I learn from posts with his friends. In October he says he has been throwing hay for 5 days and will be glad to be finished. Doug tells him what my grandmother used to say "hard work never hurt anybody." "Hang in there." He responds that he loves it and has fun doing it. He posts things from good times and bad with many posts to family and old friends. They discuss the fun they used to have and that they would like to visit, but he also posts that there is nothing for him in Princeton.

He realizes the lure of the drug culture here. In November, he thanks God that he is out of jail for the first Thanksgiving in 3 years. He is not with us, but will be soon. He posts to his Mom. "Love you Mom. Thanks so much for sticking by me when God himself knows you should have washed your hands of me long ago." She posts, "can't wait to hug you. Love you more than you will ever know." He posts, "I know, that's the main reason I feel bad for letting you down so much." Later, he says "when you turn it over to God, you know everything is taken care of."

I post a picture of Russell and his Mom from 20 years ago. Beth says "hard to remember that big boy being so little. Rotten as he was cute!" Others post, "Oh how precious! Russell was adorable and Beth was beautiful!" On his birthday Beth posts, "Happy 22nd birthday to my first baby. Praising God for the changes in your life and looking forward to see what wonderful things are in store for your future." Other posts, "I can't believe he is 22. He looks like he is only 15. He will be glad about those young looking genes one day." "I'm so glad to hear Russell is doing good. I'll pray for continuing strength and growth." "I knew he would grow up to be a nice young man." He tells his Mom that she is the best Mom and she responds that she tries. She says he is an awesome handsome son who she is very proud of. His stepmom Anna says that she is proud of him for stepping up and being the man his mom needs him to be. She knows it's hard, and knows he will be a good man. She says she loves and misses him very much. I'm sure that she is reminded of Hank when

Mary Feuchtenberger

she sees Russell's photos. So many people post how much he looks like his Dad that they can hardly believe it. One comments "they are twins!" Another says, "you are your Dad's spitting image!"

He says he hears that all the time. His cousin Kerry tells him that Hank was very proud of him and that he always wanted better for him. He wanted him not to do as he had done. Russell agrees that his Dad wanted him to do good and not go in his footsteps. He says that for awhile, he was going down the same trail, and his Dad will be glad he changed paths. Mark posts, "YOU ARE THE MAN RUSSELL!"

We have never met these saints from Texas who are caring for and teaching Russell about our Heavenly Father, but by December 12, 2013 they have traveled 1500 miles to arrive in Princeton WV! It is the day before Russell's 22nd birthday, an event he almost didn't reach. Thank you God! We do our usual guest dinner of steak, manicotti, spinach salad and rolls for Beth's family plus the director and his daughter and Russell and 2 other students in the program for a total of 11 people. Eric and Shawna are, understandably, not ready to see Russell. Beth brings her son a birthday cake and the celebration begins! Immediately, we have a great connection with these visitors. Russell looks healthy and very happy, and we all have lengthy conversations. His little sisters show huge smiles and are happy to see their big brother! The house is decorated for Christmas with a fresh cut Frasier fir tree and eight small artificial pink feather trees and lots of bling!

The Texans enjoy this visit and jokingly ask for snow, which is lacking. Several of them have never seen snow. They are staying in a nearby motel and the next day have car trouble and are in need of a mechanic. Of course, Doug is the man for the job and is happy to help. He also provides snow by means of financing a trip to a local ski resort for them. They enjoy it and did see snow, some real and some man-made, but it wasn't the best WV weather for snow seekers. We had one more dinner together and enjoyed this blessing of time with Russell and his Texas family. Doug posts that he enjoyed their visit and "God Bless, good luck and thanks for what they've done for you. We love you and are pulling for you to continue to be one of their success stories!"

Soon, it will be another Christmas without him, but he is in a good place. I send a few small gifts, but nothing special. We post Merry Christmas on social media. I tell him I am frying bacon and can't help but think of how many pieces he could eat...and wish he was here with family for sausage gravy. We know that we will see him soon, because his court date is planned for March.

Again, we keep in touch by social media and see his chats with old friends and family: "Blessed bro, I got saved July and been in Texas for almost ten months, been clean over a year. Was locked up and my mom called the guy at this halfway house/work camp if he would take me and he said yeah, so as my plea the courts sent me to long term rehab and I landed here, if I didn't come here I would be doing my same old thing." His friend understands and comments that he also got saved and it has been smooth sailing since then. He'd like to see Russell if he gets back in town. Russell responds "before, I couldn't stay out of jail long enough...I have God on my side now, so I know who and what to turn to when times get rough, and He will get me through it."

I think of the hymn "Amazing Grace" and praise God. This hymn is recognized as one of the favorites of all time. According to Wikipedia, the hymn writer was John Newton. He was a slave trader on a ship and was known for vile language and reckless behavior. During one violent sea storm he called out to God for mercy. Though spared, he continued his sinful life of trading slaves for several years before beginning to study Christian theology. Amazing Grace was written to illustrate a sermon in 1773 and later put to music. I introduced my grandchildren to this hymn, by listening to Rhema Marvanne's beautiful rendition, but most any version is soul inspiring:

```
Amazing Grace how sweet the sound that saved
a wretch like me!
    I once was lost but now am found, was blind
but now I see
```

'twas grace that taught my heart to fear, and grace my fears relieved;

How precious did that grace appear the hour I first believed.

When we've been there ten thousand years, bright shining as the sun, we've no less days to sing God's praise than when we first begun.

Russell has experienced amazing grace and is on a positive course for the first time! "Coffee, then I am going for a run and hitting the weights. I have had one hard road in life, but no one chose it, but me, and I wouldn't go back and change a thing about it; especially when it brought me to where I am today." Later he posts that he has too much on his mind, so he is going to go to bed and pray. Wow! He is finally taking his grandmother's advice! I text that I am praying for him and for everyone in rehab. Prayer is the answer for every need. Thank you Lord! Pray without ceasing.

I saw my friend, Jim, today. I used to see him several times a week in my vigorous antiquing and flea marketing days, but had not seen him in 7-8 years. He and I always shared our Christian faith, and today was not different. As we began reminiscing we both mentioned that we felt God's presence! I had this same experience recently with Tom when we shared our faith at the flea market. The spirit is there when you join with others in Christian fellowship. You will know and feel It, and It is POWERFUL!

I am enjoying a cool July evening on our porch. The pink geraniums and white alyssum are in full bloom. The flowers are gorgeous, and I remember a funny compliment on similar flowers from years ago. The O'Dell children from next door were visiting and said that their Mom had told them that the flowers on my porch were artificial because real flowers couldn't be that gorgeous and overflowing. God gave them to me, and they are exceptional....and they are real! I also enjoy Bob and Reba's flowers across the street. I am reclining outside and the wicker couch suits me. The kids use the swing with the heart cut outs, and all of it reminds me of the home with a porch where I grew up.

Groundhog Day in West Virginia

I am counting my blessings. We had a fabulous church service with a great message on love and fruit of the spirit. Galatians 5:22-23 discusses the fruit of the spirit. Love, joy, peace, patience, kindness, goodness, faithfulness, gentleness and self control were all listed on the church bulletin as fruit of the spirit. My thoughts are that these all are tremendous attributes for walking in the spirit, and I will seek these traits. Can you imagine mankind maintaining the fruit of the spirit? What a blessing that would be. The church music was outstanding with a solo of "He Touched Me" and piano playing straight from Heaven. Our church has been blessed with the amazing talent of Laurel as choir director and pianist!

One by one, see what God has done! Russell is on my mind, and I know that God has his back. They probably had a fabulous church service today in Texas. Did you? God wants us to have fellowship with other Christians! Many people are slow to take that first step to church, but I urge you to attend regularly. Sleeping late on Sunday morning is a favorite alternative for many and was, at one time, for me. When you work 5-6 days a week, it may be hard to give up your time. I used to very reluctantly wake up and get the family ready for church. I am selfish with my time, but it is actually a form of tithing... the more you give, the more you get! More free time!

We had a terrible rainstorm this morning, and I considered missing church, but WOW--look at what I would have missed--such joy in The Lord! Time is one of the most important things to give to God and loved ones and to everyone! And, God has already rewarded us today with the worship service and with our granddaughter's visit this evening. We are praying for her so much and want her to serve our Lord. We want that for you, too, and for ourselves! See what God has done!

Back to posts from Russell as he nears his March 2014 court date: "It's not about where I have been; it's about where I am headed." He posts another persons' message: "I woke up today in my bed, not in a cell, not in a casket, not in a hospital, so I have to thank God for another unpromised day." He says it is freezing in Texas (30 degrees), but it is below zero wind chill in WV. He chats with his stepdad's sister, and she compliments him on his progress. He thanks her and says "I can now say I over came my past; times get super hard and it is a miracle that I even got another chance for real." She says "keep your faith in your heart and don't let nothing or nobody bring it out....it's a beautiful life without all that mess in it. Life is getting too short." "I'm out of jail and still living off ramen noodles. I hate it.Lol!" I remind him that I had brown beans every day as a kid. With deep hurt, I recall the newscast depicting the Syrian children, victims of war, starving and eating grass and weeds. What can we possibly complain about compared to that?

February 6, 2014. "Thanks to everyone who has been with me through all my ups and downs and still staying by me." We are surprised to learn that the Texas director has been given an early court day of February 13 for Russell. It is a 1500 mile trip, and we feel blessed that the director is willing to make the drive. We are not happy with the expense involved and wonder how some people manage. Doug has taken a job after retirement, and it has eased the financial burden of Russell's care, but we are ready for his year of rehab to be over. They arrive on February 11 just as WV is preparing for a major winter storm. Snow amounts of 10-12 inches are predicted to begin the next afternoon. We have received a tremendous amount of prayer asking that the Lord guide what is best for Russell's situation. Our hopes are that the felony will be reduced to a misdemeanor or thrown out. However, we are advised by the prosecuting attorney's office that it cannot be changed from a felony. We will leave it in God's hands. Eric tries to ease the court decision with a letter:

To Whom It May Concern,

I am Russell's uncle, Eric Feuchtenberger. I filed the charges that Russell is currently facing. At the time of the incident, Russell was badly addicted to drugs. He was not the kid who I helped during his rough teenage years, who lived with my family, who played with my daughter, and even helped around the house. He was someone I didn't know, and I'm glad that I filed those charges. It got him off the street and into rehab. Before Russell became addicted to drugs, he was a good person, and now I hope he can be that again. After talking to the rehab director, my parents, and my sister about Russell's progress, I believe he can change his life into something worthwhile. I would like to see his charges dropped or reduced to a misdemeanor, so that it may be easier for him to move forward without the burden of felony charges on his record. Thank you, Eric Feuchtenberger.

Russell stays the night with us while the director stays in a local motel. After three long days on the road, it is a welcome relief for both of them. Early the next morning, the director picks Russell up to go and talk with his probation officer. Fearing the imminent storm, court plans are changed and Russell is to appear before the judge that morning. Eric is summoned and fortunately, was nearby, when normally he would be miles away and unable to be reached. The judge rules that he will put the felony charges on deep freeze for a year. Russell is to return to Texas and appear back in court February 13, 2015. The director will report on his conduct. We are pleased that the felony is on hold. Russell is glad, but disappointed. He had expected to be released at the end of March, since that was the original rehab term. However, it is wonderful to know, that with good behavior, he will no longer have a felony.

Russell was hoping to leave the rehab program sooner, and it will be hard for him to remain for another year, if he cannot drive and cannot get a job. They begin their journey back to Texas late that afternoon. During the night 12 inches of snow falls and 3 more inches the next day. It is such a blessing that the court met a day early. The Lord has a hand in everything. We had prayed that God would guide what was best for Russell. He was hoping to be free and allowed to go where he wanted, and had communicated with a woman friend in Myrtle Beach. She had offered him a job and a place to stay. Longing for total freedom, it was Russell's plan to go there and not return to Texas. However, he did say that he realized this was not God's will. Before he left, Doug loaded up the scooter we had purchased for him to use when he was working here. It is hard for a 22 year old to be in the boonies of Texas without a ride, so possibly the scooter will give some fun and freedom. We are continuing to pray for guidance and safety for the director and Russell. They travel through some bad weather, but make it back safely to the Texas sunshine. Thank you God!

Later in the week, I spoke with Eric about the court appearance. He said that it is extremely rare for him to be in his office on a Wednesday. But, the court called him that morning and said he needed to be there ASAP to testify regarding Russell. He was able to get there just in time for the hearing. Just 2 days before, he was told that he was not needed and that the felony could not be dropped. God is mighty and all powerful! We prayed for what is best because we did not know what was best. Seemingly the court did an about face and the charges were dropped for now. Eric said that a burden was lifted from him. He had not seen or communicated with Russell since their last court date when he was sentenced over a year before. This recent meeting was the beginning of restoration of their relationship.

Russell accepts being in Texas again, but begins to long for home. He swears me to secrecy in texting his unhappiness. The following texts reveal his agony: "Get me out of here before I get myself out really granny. I was really planning having this place completed when I went to court and they gave me another year and it just put me in a depression and gave me stress that I really can't handle. I CAN'T." I tell him that I will check into some trade schools and see if the director will offer his approval. Part of the court's plan was for him to enroll in classes. He responds "won't do any good, the director won't let me do anything. You all just don't understand....I honestly just don't care anymore. I mean I care, but not about this place. I am fed up and ready to move on whatever, even if I have to do my time." I respond that I care and am still looking for a school. He asks me not to tell anyone how unhappy he is. I tell him to pray and he says that he prays a lot, but his prayers don't work. I tell him they work in God's time. He posts to Kerry "it's hard and I've felt like throwing in the towel a few times. I had to call my mom and granny to boost my motivation sometimes. It's hard, real hard.

His post in early April:"I've been stressed out a little bit lately. I was almost to the point of throwing in the towel until I sat back and thought of everyone that wants to see me fail, so failure is no option for me...feeling determined." Many friends post encouragement. His cousin Kerry says "I am very proud of you and know you can do it. You're too stubborn not to. It's in the blood." Russell agrees and says that he looks too much at the negative and is working on looking at the good. She posts "we all struggle with that and trust me, you've got this. The good always outweighs the bad in life and God has you, so keep faith. Stand strong. Don't ever give up!" Wow! What an amazing statement to provide positive reinforcement! Thank you God! Kerry also tells him that when he was born Hank cried with joy and happiness, and she knows he is smiling down on everyone. Many friends say they are proud of him and to keep his head up and follow through.

I spend hours on the computer looking for a school and finally find a school of excellence about 3 hours from Princeton. It has a program to train heavy equipment operations, and that may be acceptable for Russell. There is a Narcotics Anonymous group there that would be good for staying clean, so hopefully, the director will agree to this. Beth has found another good option about the same distance away. We both pray for guidance. Again we go forward in church and ask for prayers and for the elders to gather. From the Bible Numbers 6:24-26 NKJV

Mary Feuchtenberger

The Lord bless you and keep you;

The Lord make his face to shine upon you and be gracious to you;

The Lord lift up his countenance upon you and give you peace.

As our church service ends each Sunday, we see this scripture on the front screen. What a wonderful departure message...brings a smile and I feel blessed!

Notes 21
(Discord)

Russell continues to ask me about finding a school, possibly even in Texas, so he will have something to fill his time. He is becoming restless. Without a drivers' license, he is unable to work and also has a language barrier. They are so close to Mexico that many people do not speak English, and to find a job, he needs to speak Spanish. He is stuck. The director has said he would find a school, but seems to be on slow speed. Finally, I decide to talk with Russell's probation officer. I visit him in his office, and he advises that the director has to approve Russell's activities. I express unhappiness with the courts' decision to leave him in Texas another year. What the judge did not realize when he sentenced him is that we are making monthly payments for Russell's care. How can they enforce that? We had agreed to one year and are ready to quit sending money.

I decide to write a letter explaining this to Russell's lawyer. I also believe that we should have input on a school. I have been a teacher and researched many schools trying to find the best fit. It seems unfair not to have a say in Russell's education. Be assured that we are all very pleased for him to be in Texas and would like to leave him there. But, at some point he needs to move forward. The crime he pleaded guilty to was of robbing his uncle of $300.00 and assaulting him. (Yes, he is guilty of many other untold crimes, but not prosecuted and I would never defend him, but he was a different

Mary Feuchtenberger

person then). He has served 4 1/2 months in jail and 14+ months in rehab with 10 more months required. He deserves his sentence and then some, but it is hard to understand given the crimes of others and their time served.

Russell begins talking about buying a motorcycle. That is always his dream, but we feel no obligation to finance it. The director talks with Doug and asks that we do this for Russell. He says that it will be a "loan" and Russell will pay us back with money he will make on a wood chipping business there. He says that Russell isn't ready for school, but a motorcycle is the first step in assuming responsibility. I am surprised at this request, so I text the following message:

"We are thankful and praise God for you and your organization. We are aware that Russell still has problems maintaining appropriate behavior, and while we want to contribute to his care, it is becoming increasingly difficult. We know that he is not aware of the financial hardships that we have in order to provide monthly payments for him. With recent work hours for Doug being cut, it is our hope that Russell's work for you can lower the amount that we send each month. We do not have funds to cover the cost of a motorcycle, but would consider getting a loan to pay for it if we can eliminate the monthly payments for Russell's care. In talks with his probation officer and discussing the fact that we had only agreed to a year of care, he suggested that you talked about Russell being able to work and go to school. Possibly grants and loans can ease us of his care. We are looking at a certified school of excellence about 3 hours from here that has classes beginning in July and January in welding and heavy equipment operations. We are told that he may be eligible for grants and loans and help from Voc Rehab. Also, they have a Narcotics Anonymous group near the school. We know that Russell strongly desires a motorcycle. We have given up many of our desires to help him. If he can work and pay his fees we will consider a loan for the motorcycle. Please advise us of what you feel is best for his needs. Thank you so much, Mary and Doug"

Groundhog Day in West Virginia

    The director responds that he does not feel that Russell is ready for the increased responsibility of a career and school, but he feels that a motorcycle would help him to be responsible. My reply: "we just do not have $6000.00 to loan Russell for a bike. We would have to get a loan. Doug is not working as much, and we are not comfortable borrowing money. I know that Russell gives the impression that we are well to do, and that is not the case. We live pay check to pay check like most of America. It has been hard to assist Russell, and we have our own needs. We have helped him continually since before his graduation in 2009. We are ready for him to help himself. While we wish that we could loan him the money, we cannot." His response "No problem, I understand." We are feeling very frustrated with expectations of continuing paying rehab and being asked for a motorcycle loan. I decide to write the lawyer and probation officer. I explain that we feel we should not have to continue payment, that we were unhappy with the motorcycle loan request, that it is time he learns a skill and that I would like input on a school. Russell is 22 and would like to become a productive person, but rehab personnel do not feel he is ready. I am hoping that he can begin to learn a skill other than manual labor. However, the manual labor has been great for him!

    Unfortunately, the lawyer decided to send a copy of my letter to the rehab organization. They are obviously angry and unhappy with us. It is sad since we once had so much respect for one another. They said that we do not need to continue to pay and that it isn't about the money. And, they are searching for a school. My letter was not well received, and all I can say is that their motorcycle request was not well received by us. Honestly, we know that Russell may not be ready to leave rehab, and we would love for him to stay there. But, he constantly complains to us and threatens to leave. Russell has continued to live there without our funds and without a motorcycle, through good and bad times. I will always commend the rehab organization and every person working there. Their Christian standards are top notch, and we praise The Lord for them. We love Russell and want only the best for him. He appears to be a changed person, but drug addiction is a mean mistress! From Corinthians 13:4-8 (NIV) **Love is patient, love is kind. It does not envy, it does not boast, it is not proud. It is not rude, it is not self seeking, it is not easily angered, it keeps no record of wrongs. Love does not delight in evil, but rejoices with the truth. It always protects, always trusts, always perseveres. Love never fails.**

Notes 22
(KABOOM)

As we were traveling, I realized how much I was praying without ceasing. I was thinking of things to talk to God about. I have to admit that I let my trust fail a little. Suddenly, I was agonizing. What if the beach house that I rented and paid for is a scam? Worry took over and I prayed. Matthew 6:34. **Do not worry about tomorrow. Let tomorrow worry about itself. Living faithfully is a large enough task for today.**

All but Russell would be with us. We find it sad, since he used to love riding the highest Atlantic Ocean waves. We cherish and enjoy being with family and praise our Father for those here. We awaken to a fabulous day and the perfect beach house! I glorify God for the sunshine, the glistening ocean, clear blue skies, a healthy family and for every moment with them in serene Bliss! His gifts are amazing, big and small. I had an Isaiah 65:24 (NIV) moment today. "**Before they call I will answer; while they are still speaking, I will hear.**" He gave me a bookmark today. KABOOM!!! It blew my mind to receive it so innocently, yet, I knew immediately where it came from. It was a BIG, VERY BIG GIFT, because it was so obviously from HIM! I was reading an interesting book, America the Beautiful, by Dr. Ben Carson, while sitting in a beach chair under an umbrella. Oops, I dropped my book and lost my place. I wish I had a bookmark. I scramble and find my place and resume reading. The wind blows and my pages shuffle, and I lose my place again. Oh, how I wish I had a bookmark. I again find my place and resume reading. Within a couple of minutes, a lady walking along the beach goes totally out of her way, in between multitudes of beach chairs, umbrellas and sunbathers spread on towels everywhere, to my position under the umbrella and hands me a bookmark! Gives me chills! She didn't have a clue that I needed one, but said that she passes them out to advertise a book that she has written. Her name is Carole Bellacera and the bookmark was for Incense & Peppermints.

Thank you God! I know where that bookmark came from! I text my sister-in-law Betse a note about the bookmark and she responds..."what a mystical experience from your lips to God's ears, this tiny miracle is! God is all about miracles, big and small." The hymn that ends every church service comes to mind: **Praise God from whom all blessings flow. Praise Him all creatures here below, Praise Him above ye heavenly host, Praise Father, Son and Holy Ghost. Amen** Do you see your blessings and count them one by one and thank Him. Betse told me that she discussed with a group of church friends "If you woke up tomorrow with only what you had thanked God for today...what would you have?"

I love the rainbows that are made as light passes through prisms and beveled glass. Our home is over populated with leaded glass windows that bring stunning colors and designs. My cousin Sandra gave me my first antique beveled window. I had admired the ones in her home, and we talked on the phone about their beauty. She commented that she had one, stored under her bed, waiting for just the right use, and that I could have it. She probably didn't think that I would accept her generous offer, since her St. Louis home is over 600 miles from mine. However, I have never minded a drive, so my living room is graced with her gorgeous window!

Our home is filled with a lot of "stuff" from years of flea marketing and antique dealing. A crystal chandelier purchased from a shop in Lewisburg WV reminds me of the one in the movie Pollyanna over 50 years ago. I was totally fascinated with the light fixture that showered rainbows throughout the home, never fathoming that I could own such a thing of beauty, but God remembered my amazement. Thank you God and thank you Johnny Olson from the Price Is Right! The antique shop owner said that it had come from Johnny's home there. My brother-in-law John describes it as a magical floating cloud above the dining room table. Thank you My Heavenly Father! He wants us to be happy! Move close to Him! My youngest granddaughter texted this morning, "Hi." Wow, this is a first and so sweet that she is thinking of me. We texted a little more, and it brightened my day, this blessing from God...little things, big things!

Today is Father's Day and powerful commendations have been posted. Eric says "Happy Father's Day to the coolest Dad a family could have! You have taught me so many valuable lessons and helped make me who I am today! Thanks! I love you! Beth posted: Happy Father's Day to my Superman! You're amazing in a million ways! I'm so thankful to have you as my Dad and as Pappy to my children. We love you so very much!! Thank you for being there for all of us! Russell posts: "Happy Father's Day Pap! Hope u had a good race. I bet not too many people can say their 70 year old grandpa is racing. (He is actually 69 and racing better than in his younger days. Eric is racing also and finding it difficult at times to keep up with his Dad). Thanks for everything you've ever done for me and for sticking the good and bad times out with me. Love u."

Russell also posts to Eric: "Happy Father's Day. Hope you had a good race. Thanks for supporting and standing by me when no one else did and accepting me again when you shouldn't. Love you Eric." His Uncle Eric is kind in his response. "Thanks Buddy, you're doing good, and I'm proud of you for what you've accomplished. Stay strong and the sky's the limit! Love you." Russell asks his Mom to tell Timmy happy Father's Day and to thank him for everything he tried to teach him in life. He wished that he had listened. I say my thank you to my Heavenly Father on Father's Day and every day. And, I, like my children, am immensely thankful for my husband Doug who has become a wonderful Father and grandfather. I feel very blessed that we are together to share the joy of children and also

Mary Feuchtenberger

the challenges. Cheryl Strayed, author of a favorite book and movie *Wild*, wrote a meaningful tribute on social media to her husband, and it resonated with me. She says that her children take for granted what she and her husband missed as kids "a dad whose unconditional love is ever-present, whose guidance and sacrifice and faith is in the air they breathe. This experience our children have is foreign to us, and together we often marvel over it."

That experience of an ever present biological father is foreign to me, also, and to Russell. But it is not an excuse for wrong doing or unhappiness in your life. My Mother always told me that God in heaven was my Father, since, as a young child I questioned my father's identity. It turned out that my Mom went from Princeton to Washington DC during WW II and stayed there until after the war. She met my Dad, and I guess loved him, but their marriage didn't work. When I was 18 months old, she returned with me to her parents' home in Princeton. I always heard that that my father drank and smoked too much and often didn't work. No one said anything worth hearing. Children do not want to hear negative thoughts about their parents. I know that from experience and caution you. My Dad sent me a teddy bear and called one time, when I was too far away to receive the call. That was when I was 4-5 years old, and we never heard from him again. The memory of missing that phone call hurt me for years. I longed to have a father.

I did have a grandfather, but he was not my Mom's favorite person, so she discouraged a close relationship. Still, he and I were close, and I loved him very much. He gave me the joy of books, and I have good memories of his purchases for me with Grimes Fairy Tales being a favorite. He was a former school teacher, and the one room school where he taught still stands on a farm in Elgood WV. He enjoyed reading and always doing the newspaper's crossword puzzles. He died suddenly when I was 15, and life was harder with just my grandmother and Mother. We were very poor.

When I was 14, my Dad's sister from Ohio visited and told me that he had died of lung cancer when I was five. His family had not known how to get in touch with us, so it took years for me to know that the father I prayed for every night was gone. I so much wanted a Dad, but, I knew very well that my Father in heaven was my Father who took care of me.

My Moms health was not good, but she loved me and wanted to be sure that I had all of my needs fulfilled. She was blind for much of her life, yet, she tried to be productive. It hurt to hear of the day that she had diligently worked cleaning and staining our ugly brown wooden bedroom floor. She laughingly confided to a friend that, with her poor vision, she had mistaken the molasses for the varnish. Both have an odd smell, and her good deed was disastrous! How horrible it was to have molasses cover the floor! And, how horrible it was for my Mother to be blind! She was always a God fearing woman and instilled deep Christian values in me. My grandparents were hard working and wonderful people. I know that we were a burden for them, but God provided. My grandmother said, "The older I get, the harder I work." She washed clothes with a wringer washer and hung them on the line in all kinds of weather. I remember seeing them stiffly frozen on the clothesline in frostbite weather. Clothing was sewn by an old Singer machine, and feed sacks provided much of the fabric. Gardens were planted, and most of the harvest was canned in the hottest month of August. Food was cooked each day with never a fast food meal. Money was earned by cooking and cleaning for others.

Notes 23
(Home)

We lived in an old two-story house that we rented for a small amount of money from friends. It was in decent condition, but with inadequate heating. I froze to death in the winter and slept under as many blankets as possible, snuggled very close to my mother for warmth. She showed me how to make a fold in the bottom of the blankets to keep my feet warm, and lots of socks helped. We suffered blazing heat in the summer, but many people lacked air conditioning "back then." I put my bed right in front of a window and prayed for cool breezes.

To provide a small income, rooms were rented to people who were traveling. My best friend, Billie, from those days, recently told me that her favorite memory of our home was the smell of freshly pressed sheets, starched and then ironed by a machine, called a mangle, as we prepared bedrooms for our tourists. I have wonderful memories of Billie's home. She had a beautiful Mother and a handsome Father and an adorable little sister and brother. The floors in her living room were gorgeous oak, and things were always clean and pretty. She had a swing set and nice toys. My first taste of marshmallow cream was had in her kitchen, and I couldn't believe how good it was with peanut butter on a sandwich.

I did experience one horrible taste while spending the night in her home. I developed a cough, and her Mom brought me an aspirin. I had actually never taken a pill without applesauce to help it go down. So, I decided that I would just hold the aspirin in my mouth until she left the room. Horrors! Worst taste ever!! Although it was 60 years ago, I still have trouble swallowing some pills. Billie and I tried smoking cigarettes in the old nasty coal house out back of our garage. Several kids joined us for this mischief, and I was very worried about being caught. Billie says that one of her eyebrows was burned off, and that ended smoking for her. After setting the chicken house on fire and getting in horrible trouble, I, also, gave up cigarettes.

We were fascinated by neighborhood ladies who wove beautiful rag rugs in brilliant reds, blues and most any color with white fabric using a loom in yet another building behind my home. These rugs are prime examples of the artistry of Appalachia and are still valued today. My beloved white cat often had kittens in that shed with the loom. I loved those adorable little pets, but my grandfather would quickly dispose of them saying that we could not afford to feed or keep more cats. As much as I wanted to keep them, I understood that our poverty necessitated their demise.

Much of my time was spent on swings and a trapeze in Billie's back yard. I just walked across the alley out back to be transported to heartfelt fun. Childhood memories with her are delightful! Though our lives were very different and still are, she will always be a good friend.

In our home, we had guests, known as boarders, live with us at various times. That meant that a person paid a small fee to have a bedroom in our home and to have meals with us. We had three people, at different times, that stayed a year or longer. A large sign in green neon dangled from a pole at the front of our yard and spelled out TOURIST. The house across the street where the former sheriff of Mercer County, "Coon" Fanning, lived had one too, and the house one block up from us, also rented rooms. That sign across from us was red neon. I preferred it, but our green one did the job.

Mary Feuchtenberger

This was in the fifties, and there were not many places for people to stay when traveling. Our house was on the main highway, such as it was then, and summertime was busy with all three spare rooms booked every night. Can you imagine? We only had one bathroom, and I was threatened to not dare stay in there too long. To save money and give tourists time, I took only one bath a week in a very small amount of water and for years, as an adult, resisted filling a full tub. Now, I laughingly think…I bet those kids at school didn't want to sit next to me. I will always remember a fellow classmate from sixth grade talking to another classmate about "poor little Mary Rodden." Yes, we were VERY poor, but with God's blessings, RICH! I realize that now.

Our home was one where hobos could stop by to get a decent meal, like beans and cornbread or fried eggs. My grandmother said that hobos would mark your property in some way so that other itinerants in the area might know where to ask for food. We did have a fairly steady flow of inquiries and were glad to provide. Recently, I had a man stop and ask for money for food. I told him to wait on the front porch, and I would prepare something. I fried eggs and bacon that smelled delicious, and when I went to offer it to him, he was gone. Made me mad.

If you know the Princeton area, the Maidenform was diagonally across the street from our house. All I knew about that building was that women sewed brassieres there, and that was fascinating to me. I liked to sit on the curb and watch many hard-working, beautiful women depart at quitting time each day. Nelsie, who worked at the fountain of Princeton pharmacy, lived next door. She prepared for me many a grilled cheese sandwich and vanilla milkshake at lunch break when I was in high school. Orella from up the street worked there with the pharmacist.

Sometimes, I would walk to Liggs Market for a loaf of bread or small food item. Later, that became Mills Market with Mr. Mills and several of his sons in charge. For many years, Mills Market was a favorite destination for people in Princeton. It had fresh produce and those food items you need in a rush. Corky and Violet attended our church and are missed. The market place is now home to a bank. The courthouse was two blocks away from our home, and as a young teenager, I was paid to hand out candidate flyers on Election Day. My grandmother was happy to work the polls and to count votes. These were important paying jobs.

It was amazing to watch small airplanes land and take off just a couple blocks away. I enjoyed many visits to the airport imagining what it would be like to fly. Several small planes crashed in the neighborhood over the years with lives lost and tragic memories for some. A recreation building and hospital cover that general area today. My grandmother's father lived with us and each day would vocalize, "Wonder if anyone wants to accompany me to Dobbins filling station next door to get a cold soda?" Of course, I was delighted. I still have that addiction for a cold soda and understand being hooked on a drug. Once, while chatting with my grandparents and drinking my soda in the kitchen, I saw the hugest spider imaginable just under the kitchen table. I hurried to stop that giant and as I stomped it, a million babies, or so it seemed, went running everywhere! How funny, these childhood memories are!

My great grandfather, Walter Holdren, was a much loved and memorable person in my life. He used a cane and had a distinguished white mustache. He would cut an apple in half and scrape it with a knife, feeding me juicy bites of apple fruit. He smoked a pipe that I found distasteful, but now that smell is pleasant. He doted on me and I was blessed. When someone said "Christmas is right around the corner," I said, "Let's go there!" So we walked around the corner, and he swore that he had caught just a glimmer of Santa in the distance. That is such a sweet memory. Once, when he was sick with a heavy cough, he made a home remedy containing whiskey and rock candy. Often, he shared small amounts of that rock candy with me, and I found it to be delicious, so I asked to try his home remedy. I was only five or six years old and will never forget the horror, as I took a huge drink, attempting to get a mouthful of the candy that had sunk to the bottom of the glass. That experience certainly hindered later offers from my peers to consume alcohol. I could imagine nothing worse!

My great grandfather was a former sheriff who suffered through saloon brawls, moonshining and Hatfield/McCoy squabbles in the early 1900's with Matewan and, later, Keystone WV being his job sites. Family history tells of two people that he killed due to threatening circumstances. During one murder trial, I was told that he wore his Masonic ring knowing that the judge was a Mason. He was fined $25.00 for the murder. When I was seven, he became ill while visiting his youngest daughter in Norfolk VA. My grandmother purchased a train ticket to bring him home, and I had the pleasure of joining her. The train ride was delightful and once in Norfolk, I had my first swim in the Atlantic Ocean. It was fabulous and frightening as my inner tube drifted out to sea. Fortunately, I was rescued and continue to love the ocean.

Besides my first train ride and first ocean swim, I had the joy of attending my first movie in Norfolk. "A Man Called Peter" caused me to cry uncontrollably, and reinforced my faith in God. Years later, I read the book written by Peter Marshall's wife, Catherine. It evoked the same strong emotions that I had at age seven when seeing the movie. What an astounding first trip away from home! We returned to Princeton with my great grandfather. I will always remember the total devastation that I felt when his life ended shortly thereafter, and, then, having his body in his casket on display in our home. This was the thing to do at the time, but I could never imagine continuing that practice. He was eight-four, and I expected him to live forever. He is buried with much of the family at a special hilltop cemetery in Elgood WV.

Our home was the place where tourists became friends and made a point to schedule return stays. One interesting family was deaf and dumb, but we communicated. Another time, a childhood friend of my grandmother's came for a week. They had not visited with each other since the woman had lost her eyesight at age twelve, fifty years before. I could not imagine how they still had a connection, but I do understand now. She fascinated me. Her name was Fern. I was amazed by how quickly she learned her way through our home and how she seemed so "normal." I was told that she had lost her sight because her father had syphilis before she was born. She had attended the school for the blind at Romney WV in the early 1900's and lack of vision seemed no problem for her. My own Mother lost her vision gradually when I was in elementary school, but she later had cataracts removed and could see for a few years until her optic nerves became diseased. I realize that many people have intimidating hardships. One truck driver and his wife were frequent tourists, and after his passing, his wife took over driving routes and visited when she was in the area. She delighted me by purchasing crispy cereal and marshmallows and preparing a sweet treat beyond compare.

With a big front porch lush with red geraniums, a creaky glider, an antique, black rocking chair and a welcoming swing, some of our recreation came from sharing memories there with family, tourists, and neighbors. Often, we had a glass of lemonade and sometimes a slice of lemon meringue pie or white coconut cake. We had good times, and laughter abounded! We found our tourists to be honest and enjoyed their company. Now, I cannot even trust my own grandson! Many of his friends are also dishonest due to drug use and addiction. Princeton WV has changed, as has our whole country in the years since my birth. Mercer County is rampant with drug use, but that seems true of very many places.

As a child in a family without a car, I walked everywhere and usually alone. The best and most fun destination was Wallace Street, just one street behind where I lived on South Walker. Neighborhood kids loved to gather each day, usually at Fran's house, to talk and play games like tin can alley. Two yards had swing sets that were used by many. Softball was a favorite sport, and I still smile thinking of the glide downhill while bike riding...when I could borrow one. In various homes, we listened to radio programs like Roy Rogers. He was my favorite cowboy and Billie liked Gene Autry. I sewed many dolls clothes with Carol from up the street.

Mary Feuchtenberger

I was happy to babysit for neighbors to earn money. One family only needed me one or two times a year, but I felt wealthy being paid 50 cents an hour. Soon, another well to do lady asked me to keep her energetic grandson for six hours several days a week. It was hard chasing after a three year old all day, but I was excited to be earning money. Imagine my disappointment when she gave me a dollar and said to bring back the change (10 cents). I had kept him for 6 hours, and in her mind 15 cents an hour was reasonable. After that, we established that 25 cents an hour was acceptable, but it was difficult. Sometimes, I would use curlers to style neighbors' hair and was paid 25 cents. Money was very scarce, so I couldn't be too choosey as a young girl. Many people lived in poverty as I was growing up, but most of my friends had much more than I did. I was aware of that, but thankful for what I had.

On one corner of Wallace Street, I took piano lessons, but my musical skills were lacking. The same was true when I enrolled in the band in elementary school and junior high. Band comradely is fabulous, and I wish that I could have been a better participant. I find countless salutations and accolades to my friend Charlotte's husband on Facebook. JB was a band director for many years at Richlands' High School and former students honor him at a social media fan club. I remember my band directors, Bill Lilly and Earl Erskine with much respect! I marched in many freezing cold parades, and I longed to be a majorette. I practiced for hours with an old heavy baton, yet the ability wasn't there. My best friend had amazing skill and became the band's main twirler.

As far as actual toys go, one Christmas I received a Tiny Tears doll that could drink a bottle and then pee. Another time I got a toy iron and one time a radio. At home, I colored and played with paper dolls cut from magazines. Today, I use paper for crafting and have been successful with creating Victorian style Christmas ornaments from antique paper and selling them on eBay. We kept a jig saw puzzle on a table, and I have the Chinese checkers that I used as a kid. I still like marbles and mostly search for peppermint swirls and patriotic colors. I fill jars with them and use them to hold small flags. West Virginia is known for marble making, and I have bought many on eBay from the Davis family. Pennsboro is the WV town that I took Russell to as a young teenager, so we could pick our choice of marbles. I tried to give him good memories with his Granny.

We went swimming and fishing at Claytor Lake State Park and at Smith Mountain Lake in VA. My cousin Jimmy lived at Bernard's Landing and introduced me to the pleasures of escaping to his condo there. He would smoke a turkey breast, and I would devour a sandwich beyond compare...with olives. Russell would throw in his line and be entertained for hours. Then, he could swim and play tennis or basketball.

Russell loved the movie Forrest Gump, and we watched it over and over. Like Forrest's mother, I find that "life is a box of chocolates." I have many of the best, and my life overflows with good, but Russell has taken some of my joy. Still, concern for him has brought me very close to God. Yes, I, like Corrie and Betsie ten Boom, am thankful for the fleas!

When I was a child, we didn't have a TV until I was twelve. Instead, we listened to the radio and read. Nancy Drew books were a favorite, and the library was in the Memorial Building, so I could stop on my way home from school. The first television I watched was in the 1950's at a friend's home...black and white and no remote. Local kids became family with good memories, and many of us have connected on social media.

One place that I didn't want to walk by as a child was the beer joint across the street from the courthouse. Often, my mom and I went past there on our way to the holy roller church, near Princeton Pharmacy. Men would yell things, and I held her hand tightly because I was very afraid. Also, inmates in the courthouse jail would call to us if we walked by, but otherwise the journey was safe. My Mother was determined to go to church even with the obstacle of blindness and difficulty walking. I was her assistant. I found the church frightening. People would speak in tongues and fall on the floor. It seemed to

Mary Feuchtenberger

me that the pastor screamed his sermon as he danced around talking about going to hell.

When I was thirteen, I choose my own church and was baptized at First Baptist Church on Mercer Street. A special young woman taught Sunday School and encouraged Christian behavior. I enjoyed her lessons in that beautiful church with fabulous stained glass windows. I can remember the tears and trembling as I walked up that aisle to accept Christ as my Savior. Praise the Lord! First Christian Church on Straley, where we attend now, also has beautiful windows as does Westminster Presbyterian Church in Bluefield where Doug and I were married. Dr. Patterson officiated as we went after church to say our vows in 1971. Doctor Patterson was truly a much loved inspirational Christian pastor! My grandmother, always wearing her Sunday best hat, faithfully attended the Kee Street Methodist Church, but I was happy making my own decision.

Notes 24
(Princeton)

Everywhere we went required walking. GC Murphy was the favorite retail store. I never was able to purchase much, but it was fun to look. A few trips for food items were made to Kroger and Mills Market, and a favorite place for young people was the Susie Q. Kids could eat there and listen to the jukebox. Other times, they would enjoy a cherry coke and a meal at Spangler's Drugstore. Jimmie's restaurant and Ferrell's Diner in the center of town served good food and were frequented by many. My cousin Sandra and her friend Nelda lived with us while attending Concord College. They introduced me to Brock's restaurant on the far end of town. I will never forget the experience of that first pizza when I was eight or nine years old and, even today, people talk of how delicious it was.

Lloyd's Pastry is another place that people still miss and speak of how fabulous their baked goods were. Pepperoni rolls were often a treat for kids walking from the junior high for lunch. Cream horns were my favorite, and every birthday cake for Beth was purchased there. Lloyd's had delicious food that we continue to long for. They have recently published a cookbook, so others may continue their tradition.

Santon's, Nelson's, Barbakow's and Gore's were fashion shops for women, and the Stag, Kendrick's and Lynch's had fine clothing for men. Of course, my designer was my grandmother along with many hand me downs. At that time, I had a slim figure and was easy to sew

Mary Feuchtenberger

for. I even made myself a swimsuit when I took home economics in tenth grade. It wasn't the best, but I knew that if I wanted to go to the pool, no one could afford to purchase appropriate attire. I am not a seamstress and hope that I was never photographed in that awkward looking garment. I went swimsuit shopping with my friend Ann. She bought a gorgeous suit and filled it out perfectly, and I was jealous.

Many times I walked by the courthouse, past Princeton and East River Pharmacies, past SAMS (Modads), and a great little candy store to Mercer Elementary School and even walked home for lunch. Other kids attended Knob, Thorn, and Silver Springs schools. Kids used to jeer "Knobs are snobs, but Mercer worser!" Sometimes the city bus picked me up in the winter, and I would pay with a bus token. Later, I walked even further to junior high on Straley. Some evenings I walked alone in the dark to socialize at the bowling alley behind Mercer School. The Lavon and Mercer movie theaters, in the center of town, were where I occasionally met with friends. My cousin Michael recently talked of watching One Million B.C. in 1967 at the Mercer Theater and of how much he enjoyed downtown Princeton as a child. His Mom Lucille, my Mom's oldest sister, would have her husband drive her family from Lakeland, Florida to stay several weeks each summer. My cousin Connie and I developed strong bonds during this time and would write ten page letters to stay in touch between visits. I also remained close to her siblings: Sandra, Jimmy, John and Michael.

As an only child, I am blessed to have my cousins. My Aunt Doris and Uncle Dave visited often with their children Todd and Pam. We spent most holidays together. When they were moving and searching for a home, I was asked to keep their dog. If you are a dog lover, you can understand the bond that develops, and we never returned Tippy to them. Years later, I was told by Pam, how much that broke their hearts. It was explained to them that my need, as an only child in difficult circumstances, was greater than their need. Now, I hurt for them, but was very pleased with that decision. I loved Tippy!

Although I didn't have the opportunity, Gracie's pool hall and Central Grill were frequented by numerous young people in the

Groundhog Day in West Virginia

fifties and sixties. Gracie's grandson lives across the street from us now and has shared some interesting things from her place of business. He recently showed me small glasses that patrons ordered for a shot of beer. Many young men loved the chance to meet and greet and determine the best pool hustler at Gracie's.

While in my teens, friends socialized frequently on the telephone. My first memories are of having a party line which meant that other people might be heard talking when we picked up the phone. We had to take turns using the phone with these neighbors. Each home had a different number of rings to indicate a call for that family. For the most part everyone was courteous, and we soon got a private line.

I do know that I spent many hours on the phone, some with my good friend John and a majority of them with Ann. I seldom see her now, but continue to have great memories of those teenage days. When I do see her, she flashes that great smile, and we reminisce. Her son, Scott Martin, has become a talented Hollywood actor while maintaining local ties.

As I began to date, more and more people had cars. The speed demons and muscle cars of the sixties were fabulous for taking a drive and for enjoying outdoor movies. One special friend had a Chevrolet black convertible with a white top. It was a beautiful car and my favorite choice of colors even today. The first car that I had a decision in was a 1969 black GTO convertible. Was I fortunate or what? Driving a five speed like that was a special challenge with lasting memories. In learning to drive it, my foot hit the wrong pedal, and I was transported into someone's lawn. The lady of the house quickly came out to inform me that "this is a private driveway." I was just lucky that nothing and no one was hurt! My husband, Doug, speaks of a very special Studebaker Avanti and several others that he drove like the race car driver that he is. I hear wild stories of speed and mishaps. Now, young people don't know what they missed. What was your favorite parking place?

My generation enjoyed the music of the Redcoats, Collegians, and Transit Time bands at places like King's Gallery and the Hideaway. Wacky even played me music over the telephone. Dancing was a

Mary Feuchtenberger

wonderful way to socialize and develop relationships. I'm pretty sure that my first "date" was with Max, and we went to a dance at the Memorial Building when I was in seventh grade. Kids today seem to miss a lot of the best things in life and often are too quick to rush into sexual experimentation without a loving foundation. I pray for Christian values for our young...and for everyone.

An organization of hard working and caring people, Princeton Renaissance Project, is now in an ongoing process to refurbish the Lavon Theatre and downtown Princeton. Recently completed, fabulously painted murals cover many of the buildings and the city is reaching out to artists and musicians. Reunions of classmates are encouraged with the return of cruising Mercer Street on select weekends. Much enthusiasm is shown as friends discuss plans to visit and to cruise. Back in the eighties, many kids drove this main drag and enjoyed the comradely. However, it may have gotten too large and too loud for city residents comfort, and it was banned. A former student of mine instigated this reunion of past times, and its' revival is heartwarming! She is a child of God with a disabled daughter. It is a tremendous blessing that she is working for her hometown, despite living miles away. Both of my children remember fun times visiting while cruising downtown.

In 1963, my grandparents, Mother and I moved to Thornton Avenue. I was a junior in high school and unhappy about the move. It gave me a longer walk to everywhere and the house was in need of repair. I was embarrassed by it. There was little that we could do to improve our situation in life. We made do. Usually, I rode the bus to high school, but walked up and down that long Fifth Street hill many times. A car would have been nice, but my health had to have been helped with the walking. I attended high school on North Walker Street and was always proud of that school. The teachers were top notch, and I worked hard to stay on the honor roll. Chemistry was one of my toughest classes with Mr. Durr. If you couldn't answer a question, he would say, "don't just sit there: sing a song, stand on your head, wiggle your ears, do something!" I'm sure that he is the reason that I got an A in college chemistry! When President Kennedy was killed, I was in Mr. Durr's room to hear the announcement. That still is an unbelievable event in the lives of the children of the sixties!

Later, when I enrolled in Concord College in Athens WV, I walked to catch the city bus or rode with friends. David Pedneau, a published author of mystery stories, often drove me. He had an antique car that wasn't too dependable. One horrible event occurred with a gallon of milk overturning in it and the smell lingering and lingering and lingering, until he had to get a new car! He was my dance partner in a twist contest at the Lavon Theatre "back in the day." David was an intelligent, kind person, who left this earth, shockingly, way too soon due to a heart condition. I had the honor of teaching his daughter Holly a few years back.

The sixties, for me, were drug free. I never knew anyone who used illegal drugs and barely knew anyone who drank alcohol... except my grandfather who had a problem at times. Princeton had a good work force with the Virginian/Norfolk Western Railroad and later, North American Rockwell providing jobs. I felt that Princeton was a good town to live in. Today, we have the needs of many towns...more jobs and less drugs.

I know that my safety and provisions as a child were provided by God, and I praise Him! My Mother always prayed, and I am blessed. We need to be a blessing to others with our prayers. Take time to be close with God and ask for your need, and ask for evil to be taken away. This should be ongoing with time given to our Savior. He will reward you! You will have a marvelous life!!!!! Young people are constantly temped to begin the use of illegal substances from their friends and from their enemies. Pray specifically for the person perpetuating the evil, pray the evil be destroyed and pray for resistance to the evil! Peer pressure is there. Our small city has many cases of hepatitis and many cases of drug use. Please pray for a change!! Do not put this on the back burner. Be a prayer warrior! I ask God for our country and for EVERY person to accept Christ and to live for Him. You WILL have an AMAZING life filled with the riches of GOD and a home in HEAVEN one day. I'm looking forward to that day when I'll Fly Away, Oh Glory, I'll Fly Away!

Notes 25
(Red Moon)

In early July, Russell posts "boredom is going to be the death of me." His cousin Mark tells him to make a gratitude list of people and things he is lucky to have in his life. That is a great idea, and I do thank God each day. Sadly, Russell calls near the end of July, 2014 from Texas. He says that 3-4 other people in rehab have begun using drugs again. He confides that he is the only one there who could pass a drug test, and I have to admit that I am concerned. He is agonizing over what to do and asks for advice. These people are friends, and he is with them every day. Yet, he has told them that they need to quit or the director should be told. He is very hesitant to be a snitch, even though it may save a life. My advice, as usual, is to pray.

The following day, Beth says that she talked with Russell, and he said that the director found the others using drugs. Russell is off the hook! Thank you God! Now, I am praying for each person there including the directors. I pray for blessings on them and guidance in all they do. He texts a few days later that the other rehab guys are in jail for using coke. He is the only one left in rehab. Thank you God for Russell's resistance! I feel deep sadness for what drugs do to so many people, and I continue in prayer for them.

Russell has wanted to leave the program for quite some time. We have wondered what to do with him to get him in a good position for a job and have checked into various vocational schools.

Groundhog Day in West Virginia

The rehab director is looking at a motorcycle mechanic school that Russell requested. Reviews that I have found for this school are not the best, and the distance from Princeton is troubling. I feel that Russell will need closer moral support. We always search and try to eliminate areas that might have many drug users, but that place does not exist. We know Princeton is not an option. We were shocked to learn of the drug use in rehab, but realize that each person has to make a conscious decision not to use, regardless of the place and circumstances. And we do know, once again, prayer is the answer.

More posts show a very happy smiling Russell. People post "love your smile. Lookin good." You came a long way. I'm proud of you "His mom posts "that smile makes my heart so happy. I love you." And I say "I love your smile."

Beth recently received this wonderful message from Russell, "I know it is late, but I want you to know that I really am thankful to have a great Mom like you that helps me and supports me even though we don't get along all the time. I wasn't ever good at showing it. I do love you and am very grateful that you are my Mom. I love you very much. Even though I complain about this place, sometimes you just are going to have to listen to me. It has made me a lot better person. I even had the chance to drink tonight and everyone else did. I sat in my room and texted girls and played Xbox, so had you not found this place, hard to tell where or what I would be right now. A lot of guys that have did half of what I did don't have family that love them unconditionally like you all do me. I am very, very, very thankful. I love you, you all are the best. That's really to all of you guys."

On Eric's birthday he posts, "happy birthday to the best uncle anyone could have. Love you. Hope you have a good day." Doug posts. "Keep your goals in your mind and think positive! Nothing good in life comes easily or quickly. We're proud of the progress you've made and we love you!!! He says, "love you too, Pap."

One of the things obvious from these posts it this: positive reinforcement is mighty and family is key. If you can't use kind words, just don't say it. The tongue can be a horrible evil tool. A post on Facebook from Godly Woman Daily reminds us that 1 Peter 3:9 tells us **"Never retaliate when people say unkind things about you. Pay them back with a blessing...and God will BLESS YOU!"**

August 14, 2014 is a great day! Hurray! Russell texts that he has passed his Texas driver's test! Finally a step forward! He has hoped for this for a very long time and we are proud of him, and we appreciate rehab for following through. We know that Russell can be a difficult young man, and personnel may have hard times steering him in the right direction. This is his 17th month there.

A few days later, I received a call from a very excited young man. He is bursting with pride that the rehab director is allowing him to watch over operations there for a few days while he is out of town. And, he will be in charge of the church message. He is interested in the story of Joseph and the coat of many colors and is formulating a plan to use it for his sermon. We discuss how jealously led the brothers to think of killing Joseph and how bad it is to be jealous. Yes, Russell is bringing me to the Bible again and nearer to God, and I believe vice versa...praises to God Almighty!

I tell him to be very well prepared and to speak slowly and to prepare much more than he thinks he will need. My 30+ years of teaching allow me to give a little advice. He is nervous, and I tell him to practice. I will pray for him, and I ask others to pray for him. He tells me that I am one of God's angels, and I remind him of the power of prayer. He says yes....look at him. He has certainly been the recipient of much prayer and has come a long way! I tell him that I'm no angel, but I try to stay close to God, and I know how much God has helped him. Then, he says that I am "close to being an angel." I thank him, and I do know that I am blessed!

I am on the receiving end of much prayer recently due to terrible pain in my left arm and shoulder. Most people know what that is a sign of, and I did go to the ER and spent a night in the hospital. The stress test showed a problem, so I have visited a heart doctor and am having a catheterization scheduled. Certainly, this has made me think some about my leaving earth and has put life in the proper perspective. As my mother-in-law said to me not long before her passing, "we all want to go to heaven; we just don't want to have to die to get there or, at least, not right now."

I have begun thinking about seeing loved ones and the joys of heaven and know the ones left behind will be taken care of. Our church message this past Sunday was on the fruit of the spirit--patience. Pastor Bill talked about how God is patiently waiting for each of us to accept him. He wants us with him in heaven!

In Revelation 3:20 (NIV) he says **Behold! "Here I am! I stand at the door and knock. If anyone hears my voice and opens the door, I will come in."** He means it! All you have to do is ask. The time is coming. In Acts 2:20 God gives us a reminder. **"The sun will be turned to darkness and the moon to blood before the coming of the great and glorious day of The Lord."** We did have a beautiful blood red moon in April 2014, but no one knows when God is coming. The Bible tells us in Psalms 90:4 **a thousand years is like a day to The Lord.** Things are done in God's time not in our time.

However, we need to be ready at all times because we love The Lord and want to join Him in Heaven. Second Peter 3:10 (KJV). **But the day of The Lord will come as a thief in the night; in which the heavens shall pass away with a great noise, and the elements shall melt with fervent heat, the earth also and the works that are therein shall be burned up."** According to Romans 10:9-10 **"If you confess with your mouth "Jesus is Lord," and believe in your heart that God raised Him from the dead, you will be saved."** From (NIV) John 6:47-48 **"I tell you the truth, he who believes has everlasting life. I am the bread of life."**

I know that I am going to heaven and you can know that too. Accept Christ as your savior, ask forgiveness of sins and move close to Him.

We know of Martin Luther King Jrs.' work for equality, but he was also a pastor devoted to God's work and left many messages to encourage us in our faith. A favorite is "the purpose of life is not to

Mary Feuchtenberger

be happy, nor to achieve pleasure nor avoid pain, but to do the will of God, come what may. I just want to do God's will." I love his "I Have A Dream" speech. It is tremendously uplifting and inspiring to hear him utter those words "free at last, free at last, Thank God Almighty, we are free at last!" His work for civil rights and his devotion to God are examples for all of us. In his Mountaintop speech he says he sees the Promised Land, meaning, to me, equality for all on earth and eternity with God in Heaven.

Do you see the Promised Land? It is our future, and we never know when. I had good reason to think that it might be soon, but God blessed me with a good report on my heart tests in Roanoke. Praise The Lord! The one goal that I wanted to complete when I was sick was this book. Now that I am better, I will double my efforts.

Notes 26
(Social media)

Social media is once again a means of information about Russell in August 2014. He posts: "filling in for my pastor while he was gone--probably the shortest message the church ever heard, but I did it! He receives many compliments. Roger says, "Proud of ya my boy. Keep it up." LeAnn posts, "That's awesome Russell. There are no perfect people. You just keep striving everyday to be the best man you can be! Very proud of you!!" Danielle writes, "proud of you Russell, that's great. I'm really happy for you." Sarah says, "you're doing awesome. Keep it up!" Cody says he wished that he could have heard it, and it looks like he had it on lock. I, also, would have loved to have heard it and his Pappy posts, "proud of you! Wish I had been there to hear you. Keep up the good works! We love you!"

Russell says that the church said he did very good. He said that he was really nervous and was sweating for real, for real! Mike posts, "proud of you brother." His Mom writes, "my heart is overjoyed and you are on your way and I'm so proud. We love you so much!" I tell him that my heart is better already! Alane says what we all feel. "Wow what a transformation! This fills my heart to see you doing work for Jesus!!! Praise God!! All of us on this new grid." Kandie posts, "I hear redeemed all in your words man. It's a blessing to know all along He was there. He took us and wrote forgiven on your life. Good stuff. Amen! I am redeemed too. Can I get an Amen!"

Mary Feuchtenberger

    Russell posts that he is so glad that he has changed and Ashleigh says, "so am I and I thank God...and that Russell should be proud." He says, "I am definitely. Had it not been for God, we wouldn't be where we are today." His stepmom Anna says, "looks good babe. Yes, he'd (his Dad Hank) be very proud of you. I know it with all my heart and soul! Keep it up and stay strong." April says "that is awesome Russell. I bet you were nervous as crap! Ha ha, but you did it! Way to go! Sure that you put a lot of smiling faces! Especially God and that's all that matters!" Angie posts that she is proud of him and glad he took the right road and that many people don't do that. His Dad would be proud. Mark says "Awesome!"

    I love that people encourage Russell, and I love his testimony. "For anyone that knows the life I was living or the person I was, to the person I have become should know God works miracles! I'm still not perfect, but I'm not who or what I used to be or what I am going to be, but I'm getting better every day."

    I thank Jesus for Russell's salvation and remember the hymn honoring Him. **Jesus, Jesus, Jesus, sweetest name I know Fills my ev'ry longing, keeps me singing as I go.**

Notes 27
(Lace)

I am wading through baskets of antique lace in the form of collars, jabots, petticoats, handkerchiefs, trim...and enjoying every minute. The handwork of women from the Victorian and Edwardian Eras is cherished by me and countless others. The recent public television programs of Downton Abbey and Mr. Selfridge take us back to periods of elegant glamour and an appreciation of high fashion from earlier times.

    I began purchasing lace and fabric from estate sales and antique shops over twenty years ago with the goal of hand crafting angels with these purchases when I retired. The question is "where did the time go and why did I buy so much?"

    Many of my days have been joyous with caring for grand children, and some have been hurtful when coping with difficult young people. Russell has consumed much of my time, yet I praise God for the time and ability to care for the children of my children and know that Doug and I are blessed. And, I have made a few angels and received much enjoyment in looking at the skilled needlework of the early lace makers. When I decided to downsize my collection, I told Doug that it was like the bread and the fish.

    According to the Bible, Mark 6:41: Jesus took 5 loaves of bread and 2 fish and looked to the heavens and blessed it. He then fed multitudes and had food left over. Instead of the amount of lace

Mary Feuchtenberger

decreasing as I have sold items on eBay, it has seemed to increase. I found things that had been tucked away in the attic for years with no remembrance of seeing them before. Thank you God! He knows my appreciation of lace, and it has been fun to go through, but sad, in some ways to let go. However, I know that it is time. I am reminded of Ecclesiastes 3:1-8 (NKJV) **To everything there is a season, A time for every purpose under heaven: A time to be born, And a time to die; A time to plant, And a time to pluck what is planted; A time to kill, And a time to heal; A time to break down, And a time to build up; A time to weep, And a time to laugh; A time to mourn, And a time to dance; A time to cast away stones, And a time to gather stones; A time to embrace, And a time to refrain from embracing; A time to gain, And a time to lose; A time to keep, And a time to throw away; A time to tear, And a time to sew; A time to keep silence, And a time to speak; A time to love, And a time to hate; A time of war, And a time of peace.**

Earthly time speeds away. My hope is for every person to prepare for eternity. There is unspeakable evil in our world, and I am praying for God to take hold of those who we hear about daily, that are perpetuating their damage on others. ISIS militants beheaded American journalist, James Foley, and felt glorified in doing it and have killed and tortured many others. I cried that anyone could be so cruel and immediately prayed for the families and for the evil to be struck down. If you think that your life is bad, you may want to think again! Children and women are raped by savage devils in war-torn countries and possibly nearby. Please take the time to pray for an end to the evil and for blessings on the victims and guidance for the perpetuators. A recent Christian program with Stephen and Alex Kendrick suggested that we DEVOTE ourselves to prayer! And, I, also, saw a post credited to Martin Luther: "To be a Christian without prayer is no more possible than to be alive without breathing." God is always the answer!

Notes 28
(Granny)

Another one of those unexpected phone calls! Granny, granny--I called my lawyer and he got me a court date--10 days from now! Well, this means that I need to get my ducks in a row! He will require a bus ticket from Texas and money...this is such a strain on a continual basis. So, I check the internet for bus schedules and regulations. I can purchase a ticket online, but he has to pay a fee to pick it up and possibly suitcase fees, plus travel money for the three day trip. I appreciate Walmart's money transfer system, but have to make two trips to send funds, since his needs increase daily.

    He probably calls me ten times a day with excitement. Soon, he arrives very early Monday morning 9/22/14. And, fortunately for me, a friend volunteers to pick him up in Bluefield WV. Once here, he is overjoyed, but exhausted from sleepless travel, so a seven hour nap is in order. I awaken him to visit with his mom, stepdad and sisters at their home. Kylie loves Russell "to the moon and back" and is delighted to see her brother, and he is delighted, also. They all enjoy being together. He is happy to reunite with many friends, but we warn him to avoid those with bad habits. It is difficult to trust.

    He is gushing with happiness to be back in Princeton WV. He had been in jail for over 4 months and then, in Texas for 18 months, and longed to be home. His wonderful smile is a constant reminder of the love that I have for him. He can be a real sweetheart when

Mary Feuchtenberger

drugs are not a part of his life. He is polite, helpful and considerate with things around the house. Yet, he is a young man hoping to get out and about and become part of society again. Immediately, he reconnects with a girlfriend from his past. We like her and Russell begins staying at her place right away...not good. She is not on drugs, but, to me, it is a step away from God. Problems quickly arise, and their relationship is short lived, so he again stays with us...for a while. Soon, he begins staying with his friend Chief. We like Chief and appreciate that he seems to provide for Russell while having a wife and children to care for.

We begin searching for jobs for him and know that he will need a car. Both searches require hours of time on the computer and going to car lots. Doug takes a second job to fund the car purchase that Russell will need for work. We set limits on its use, but put the title in his name for insurance purposes. We allow him to use it to job hunt and for some visits with friends. It immediately has parts that require repair, and the needs continue with numerous fixes and more money spent. Our son had a car like this that we purchased used with 100,000 miles. It went another 150,000 miles pretty much trouble free. No such luck this time!

Russell gets a few odd jobs and begins spending time with a different girl from his past and reconnecting with more questionable friends. He has only been back in Princeton for three weeks. Our concern is increasing. His visits to our home are infrequent now. On one recent visit, I felt extreme doubt about his state of mind. He was very hyper, and I questioned him about drug use. He has a new girl waiting in the car. He becomes angry and says to just give him his car title and he won't bother us again. Doug and I discuss this change in personality and feel the need to harness his use of the car. It was purchased for transportation to work, not fun and games.

Later, that evening, Doug sees him and reminds him of the car's purpose and tells him to park it at our house for the night, but he refuses. How quickly the old Russell resurfaces! He has been back 25 days. I have already made the decision to disallow him in our home without Doug. I am again afraid of him, and my heart is aching and

Groundhog Day in West Virginia

tears falling. Psalms 147:3 tells us that God heals the broken hearted. I qualify and ask for His intervention. I know that God is the answer.

I remember Russell, just recently, praising God on social media. The devil has quickly returned to his life. This is a reminder of how important a church family is. We took him to our church on his first Sunday home and to a more youth centered church the next Sunday. He agreed to go with us the next week, but later said he was "sick" and couldn't go. This week we offer to attend a church he had expressed interest in, but he ignored our offer. His Texas church family was wonderful and without them, he feels he deserves good times as a reward for 18 months in rehab.

After defying Doug's request to return the car, he visits the next day and we talk. He says absolutely that he is not using drugs. Where have I heard that before? We would like to believe him, but have severe doubts. We discuss the possibility of his returning to Texas. He says he will go if he can take the car. We say no.

I never planned to write a book. I am not a writer. Words flow fabulously from several of my family members and friends, and I advise them to write a book. It hasn't happened...yet, but hopefully it will. My mission in writing has been cathartic. A wonderful side effect would be for even one person to accept Jesus Christ or to be helped in some way by reading about the rewards of Christian living. I know that I am going to heaven, and I want that for each of you. What a world we live in! It is full of sin and the absence of living for God. I am very guilty of many sins, but I am forgiven and you can be too. Please ask God to come into your heart and to cleanse you. The absolute, only way to happiness is through the acceptance of Jesus Christ. So many turn away and seek joy through sin. I've been there, done that. I tell my loved ones that they can have a marvelous life, if only they believe. I want each of you with me in heaven. Not many will be there, but think about it. Join me!

Notes 29
(Heroes)

There are several life stories of people who have endured beyond belief life challenges and moved forward to honor God in remarkable ways. Many may know of them, yet, I want to be certain that Russell and my other grandchildren are aware of their lives and know that difficulties can lead to blessings.

In her book, the Hiding Place, Corrie ten Boom relates tremendous life hardships that leave tears streaming from my eyes. Her family made the decision to hide Jewish friends in their home in Holland during World War II. Eventually, the Nazis discovered their hiding place and imprisoned Corrie and other family members. Corrie and her beloved sister Betsie were taken to Ravensbruck in Germany. This women's prison was known for having the worst living conditions possible, and many people were tortured unmercifully day and night. Corrie and others imprisoned there heard the agony of hell on earth as women in neighboring barracks were beaten. It was hard for Corrie to maintain her deep faith, yet Betsie persevered with strong encouragement for everyone.

A Bible had been smuggled in, and many women received comfort from Bible studies done in secret. Upon discovering their jail beds covered in countless fleas, Corrie wondered, with dismay, how to survive. Betsie gave the solution from the Bible: 1 Thess: 5-18 (NIV) **"Rejoice always, pray constantly, give thanks in**

Groundhog Day in West Virginia

all circumstances; for this is the will of God in Christ Jesus." So the women thanked God for being together and having Bibles and for so many prisoners to hear God's word. And, Betsie thanked God for the fleas!

Corrie certainly didn't think that was necessary, but Betsie said "give thanks in all circumstances." So, reluctantly she did, but felt sure that her sister was wrong. Later, it turned out that those fleas were a blessing! None of the prison guards wanted to go into the rooms because of the fleas. This gave the women freedom from possible harm and allowed the Bible studies! Amazing faith! By the end of the war, Betsie had died, but Corrie went on to inspire the world with speaking engagements, book writing and a movie about her life in "The Hiding Place." Corrie had a favorite quote from her sister, Betsie, and it applies to many life struggles--"there is no pit so deep that HE (God) is not deeper still."

Another outstanding servant of God during WWII was Irena Sendler. She was a social worker whose job was to check children for the disease of typhus. This allowed her access to Jewish infants and children who would possibly be killed. She smuggled, with the help of others, 2500 children to safety and kept a record of their names buried under a tree in her yard with the hopes of later reuniting them with their families. But, by war's end, many parents had been killed, and most all children were placed in foster homes or adopted. Before the end of WWII she was caught and the Nazis broke many of her bones and brutally beat her. Still, she did not divulge the names of assistants or foster families. What a servant of our Lord!

The story of Louis Zamperini is documented in the book Unbroken by author Laura Hillenbrand and the movie Unbroken by filmmaker Angelina Jolie. Both are well worth your time. Louis was a feisty young man who pushed many limits on correct behavior, but went on to impress the world in Olympic competition. Later, in World War 2, he enlisted in the Air Force and survived a shattering plane crash in the Pacific Ocean. He and 2 others floated on a raft for 47 days surrounded by hungry sharks. Their health plummeted without sufficient food and water, and one man died. Louis and his

Mary Feuchtenberger

friend were rescued by Japanese soldiers to face, what seemed to me, a fate worse than death in a prisoner of war camp.

Louis became the favorite prisoner to torment for over 2 years, and the reenactment in the movie is heart breaking to watch. He was rescued at the war's end and returned to the United States to endure nightly horrors of memories. Alcohol became his best friend, and after his marriage, his sickness became too much for his wife. She filed for divorce. However, after attending a Billy Graham crusade, she offered to delay the divorce if Louis would accompany her to Billy Graham's meeting. This experience totally transformed Louis as he accepted Christ, completely gave up alcohol and became a devout Christian and motivation speaker!

God does work miracles! Move close to Him! There are countless testimonies of people in total darkness seeking an answer and finding the light through Jesus Christ. I pray for that for every person. Ask him to come into your heart.

Notes 30
(Groundhog Day)

Once again, our grief is massive from a drug tormented grandson. He did appear at our doorstep to get ready for church as we had requested, but before time to leave, he had a text and said he needed to see someone and would meet us at church. He arrived 5 minutes or so late, but we were glad for him to be there. We enjoyed the sermon and felt it was appropriate for our feelings. From Ezekiel 37:1-2 our pastor talked about being in the valley of very dry bones and the feeling of hopelessness. We do sink into despair when we find once again that our grandson has succumbed to drug use. However, in Ezekiel, the Lord breathed spirit and transformed those bones.

While we want Russell's redemption to be immediate, we have to know that it will be in God's time. He texted a little during church and was actually requesting gas money from his Mom and then from us as soon as church was over. I said that I would be upset if Doug gave him more money. It is never ending, and Doug is an unknowing, willing participant.

Soon, upon our arrival at home, he appeared at the door to INSIST on gas money. He was angry with me for telling his Mom and Doug not to give him any. I've had this fight before and am worn out with paying for drugs. He packed his bags and said that he was leaving for NC and had to have gas to travel. Finally, Doug gave him 5 gallons that we had for mowing. He was ranting and raving to where I could hardly deal with it and felt fearful. I shook for over an hour and, of course, my tears are flowing, and I am talking to God.

I love my grandson. My heart hurts so much for him. Sometimes, I try to send him telepathic messages, since we no longer speak. The message is: I love you, I love you, I love you! I pray for God to guide him and each of us to only do what is good and right in His sight. I ask our Lord to take all our evil away and to guide others and to take their evil. Russell said that this town is definitely not the place for him. He lamented that he can't find a job and never has any money. That is so untrue, since he actually has had quite a bit of money from working for us, and considering his only expense is gas for his car, he is well off. He could earn even more, but doesn't like the "women's work" that I offer. He possibly will be back in jail soon. We are in disbelief at the brevity of his freedom from drugs, but we know that God is in control. A recent text from Beth brought me to my knees. She was preparing to leave for work at 5:45 A.M. and hurried to her car and began to pull out when she heard a loud voice "MOM"…scared her to death, and she said that she screamed so loud that she woke a friend a half block away. Russell was lying down in the back seat covered in blood and with a black eye and sore ribs. He was in agony, but didn't want to be taken to the hospital. His appearance frightened his sister Kylie. This is the life of a druggie and their family.

It didn't take Russell long to move away from GOD. It is, without a doubt, Groundhog Day in WV.

EPILOGUE

I asked Betse to proofread this book, and I am eternally grateful to her. She corrected grammatical errors and made a few suggestions on content. The ending did not quite suit her, and I had felt uneasiness with it myself. I'm sure that many understand the character of the disease of addiction. But, be assured that healing does come through Jesus Christ! Russell is His child, and we are comforted by our Heavenly Father! I have turned it over and will see recovery in God's time.

In our church service today, Pastor Chris emphasized that we serve an ALMIGHTY GOD! Know that EVERY request can be fulfilled and that HE is in charge! Through Him all things are possible.

NKJV: Isaiah 9:6 ..."**And He will be called Wonderful Counselor,**

Mighty God, EVERLASTING FATHER, Prince of Peace."

ABOUT THE AUTHOR

Mary Feuchtenberger is a retired teacher who lives with her semi-retired husband in southern West Virginia.

She enjoys being a crafter in the heart of Appalachia and feels blessed to live in the beauty of the mountains.